INDIAN VEGETARIAN COOKING

Other titles in this series

Greek Vegetarian Cooking
Italian Vegetarian Cooking
Mexican Vegetarian Cooking
Oriental Vegetarian Cooking
Vegetables the French Way

INDIAN

VEGETARIAN COOKING

MICHAEL PANDYA

HEALING ARTS PRESS
Rochester, Vermont

Healing Arts Press
One Park Street
Rochester, Vermont 05767

Library of Congress Cataloging-in-Publication Data

Pandya, Michael
   Indian vegetarian cooking / Michael Pandya.
     p. cm.
   ISBN 0-89281-342-3 :
   1. Vegetarian cookery. 2. Cookery, Indian. I. Title.
TX837.P27 1989
641.5′636--dc20
                                                        89-15596
                                                        CIP

Printed and bound in the United States

10 9 8 7 6 5 4 3 2 1

Healing Arts Press is a division of Inner Traditions International, Ltd.

Distributed to the book trade in the United States by Harper and Row Publishers, Inc.

Distributed to the book trade in Canada by Book Center, Inc., Montreal, Quebec

Distributed to the health food trade in Canada by Alive Books, Toronto and Vancouver

CONTENTS

DEDICATION
To Dearest Mausi and Respected Mausa ji —
May their souls rest in eternal peace!

# Acknowledgements

Let me start by paying heartfelt tribute to my dearest mother — the goddess of the kitchen who introduced me to the splendours of Indian cooking — and to my revered father — the value of whose general teachings can hardly ever be exaggerated. Their blessings have given a new direction to my life.

Around Christmas of 1983, I flew to India to do some research for this book. Naturally, I went to many places and talked to many people during my stay. Having sharpened my taste buds with some favourite *chaat* dishes at Kanpur — my home town — I visited a bit of ancient India. In addition to feasting my eyes on the famous temples and *ghaats* at Benares — the centre of Indian traditions and vegetarianism, and visiting the refreshing sights of Sangam — the confluence of three rivers (one of which is invisible) and the University at Allahabad, I absorbed the arresting aroma in the traditional eating places there and tasted some real Indian cooking!

The purpose of my brief stopover at Bombay — the showcase of modern India — was to talk with some cookery experts and get a taste of the food that common folk enjoy; the desire to meet the top stars of the Indian film industry or visit the site where they intend building the seven-star hotel was only secondary! I then did a quick change of scene and visited the centres of sophistication in food and cosmopolitan cuisine, i.e., Agra, Lucknow, and Delhi, and enjoyed the national gastronomy to my heart's content. In the process, I was able to admire the exquisite beauty of the Taj Mahal at Agra, have a leisurely limousine drive through the fashionable *Hazrat Gunj* at Lucknow and enjoy the novelty of rickshaw, tonga, and scooter taxi rides while sightseeing at the Red Fort, *Jama Masjid,* and the Parliament Building at Delhi.

Paucity of space prevents me from naming individuals; however, may I offer my sincere thanks to all who made my whirlwind study tour so delicious and enjoyable! It was indeed very encouraging to see the enthusiasm for vegetarian and wholefoods soaring in India.

Thanks to Heather Morgan, my typist, for working hard and efficiently to get the material ready on time. She proved beyond doubt that she is not just a pretty face, and also enabled me to preserve my reputation for meeting publishers' deadlines. Thanks are also due to Caren Watkins, who gave valuable assistance to Heather in completing the work.

I was delighted when John Hardaker, the Editorial Director of Thorsons, asked me to write this — my first — wholefood book. I hope that you will enjoy reading it as much as I have enjoyed writing it. As a matter of fact, I am already getting some reactions to this book; and they are nothing short of wholesome. If there is a demand for more wholefood books on Indian cookery, I am sure the supply will not be lacking!

M.P.

Food is a vital component of any nation's social fabric; you can almost judge a people by what they eat, and how. To India, with its population of over 800 million today, food is undoubtedly important. Luckily, India is richly endowed with natural resources; she produces a wealth of spices, a vast variety of vegetables, and tons and tons of grains; and her genius shines nowhere brighter than in the realm of cooking.

Over 4,000 years ago, the founding fathers of India's civilization first espoused the cause of vegetarianism and denounced the eating of any meat or flesh. They regarded all life as sacred and exhorted their countrymen to cook and eat the natural food products — and "whole" foods have always offered a whole new experience, naturally! They encountered no difficulty in making a convincing case that vegetarian food is humanitarian and economical; that vegetarian dishes tasted every bit as scrumptious and were as nourishing as the non-vegetarian food; and that three-quarters of the food intake of all non-vegetarians is vegetarian anyway!

Encouraged by this, the Indian chefs experimented imaginatively with the natural products and developed an unassailable mastery over vegetarian cuisine. A lot of cooking was done in the kitchens all over India, and some sensational combinations of ingredients and delectable dishes were created. By the Middle Ages, while some Western cynics were still poking fun at the food eaten by the vegetarians, because they were far from satisfied that a meal could be complete or nutritious without meat, India had become the undisputed centre of vegetarianism in the world. The culinary accomplishments of India were duly rewarded when the national Mughal courts established a convention of appointing Indian cookery experts among their top courtiers!

It may come as a surprise, but Indian vegetarians do not normally eat eggs. Milk is the star attraction of the vegetarian cooking scene. Literally hundreds of dishes are made from milk or milk-derived basic ingredients like *ghee*, *khoya*, cream cheese (*chhena* or *paneer*) and yogurt; no wonder the cow — as the main source of milk — is sacred to the Indians!

A meal in an Indian home is normally a balanced presentation — the spiced dishes and yogurt concoctions usually end up doing the balancing act! The cooks among some 400 million vegetarians of India learn the secrets of cooking their family specialities from their mothers and fathers so that they can prepare balanced meals for their families and friends. Not surprisingly, these accomplished sons and daughters can, for instance, coax the same vegetables — or any other basic ingredient — into a diverse range of dishes; each of its own particular flavour, texture and appearance! The contagion seems to be spreading beyond the shores of the Indian subcontinent; and it is no meagre satisfaction for me to witness that vegetarianism is coming of age in the West also.

Indians are firm believers that the way to the heart of one's beloved is inevitably through his or her stomach. The preparation and eating of food is therefore done with lots of fanfare, festivity and respect. If your food offering pleases your partner, you are almost there! Diversity of regional produce and local climate and distinct cooking and eating methods produce colourful ingredients and dishes — a veritable rainbow of the Indian vegetarian food firmament!

Kashmir, Punjab and the surrounding areas in the north of India are the "wheat" zones, where rice preparations take a secondary place. Madras — and indeed the whole of southern India — basks in the glory of its rice and vegetarian preparations. Coconut, tamarind and mustard oil are very much in evidence in this region's cookery; no wonder the "mild" dishes of the South are often hotter than the "hot" dishes of the North. Rice and pulse preparations are the staple foods in West Bengal on the eastern seaboard of India. Bengali sweetmeats are world famous. Gujrati and Maharashtrian dishes are the specialities of western India. Meals in this region normally start with a sweet dish and end with a rice preparation.

Central areas, like Delhi, are in a position to create what is christened cosmopolitan cuisine by picking the best offerings from the regions and adapting them into national superstars! This is an eloquent demonstration of India's unity in diversity. All in all, India's vegetarian cuisine can unfurl new horizons and add a new dimension to your culinary prowess. Apply a little imagination and ingenuity, and you will be ready to entertain the prince or princess of your dreams!

Bon appetit!

CARDIFF
1985

Michael Pandya

Chauke ke Bartan

The Tools of an Indian Kitchen

Try to create a total Indian atmosphere in your kitchen by using the utensils commonly found in an Indian kitchen; most of them are easily available from many Asian corner shops. Although many western utensils are quite suitable for Indian cooking, using the typical Indian tools will give you confidence and will put you in the right mood to get cooking! I list below some components of the Indian kitchen:

BHAGONA: A metal cooking pot; a sort of heavy saucepan. Slightly different-shaped deep cooking pots are known by the names of *batloi* and *degchi*.

CHAKLA-BELAN: These are like the bread board and rolling pin of the West; used for rolling out pancakes of pastry and dough.

CHAMCHA: A metal scoop that looks like a ladle; used for serving curries and soups.

CHHALNI: Wooden or metal sieves used for straining liquids and flours.

CHIMTA: A pair of flat, long tongs; normally used for picking up food items from direct heat and turning over *chapaatis*.

JHANNA: A long-handled spoon with a perforated disc at the end; normally used for draining food items out of a *kadhai* or deep fryer.

KADDUKAS: A traditional grater, standing on four feet; used to produce many types of large and small gratings.

KADHAI: A deep, wide-mouthed metal pan with round handles on both sides. It resembles a Chinese *wok* and is widely used for deep frying.

KARCHHI: A metal stirrer; a spoon with a long handle and a flat disc at the end used for stir frying and turning over dry vegetable preparations.

KATORI: A small metal bowl. Several of these are used per person to serve curried or liquid dishes with a traditional meal.

KHALLA-MUSARIA: A cast iron cousin of the pestle and mortar. It is also known by the name of *imaamdusta*. Normally used for pounding hard ingredients.

SIL-BATTA: A traditional Indian grinder of chutneys, herbs and spices. It consists of a pair of treated stones. The ingredients are placed over a large stone slab with a rough surface (known as the *sil*) and are then pressed by a small round stone with a treated rough surface (known as the *batta*).

TARAAZU: A pair of scales for weighing ingredients.

TAWA: A cast iron griddle, available with or without a handle. Generally used for making *chapaatis* and *paraunthas*.

THAALI: A metal salver, sometimes with built-in bowls; used for serving a traditional Indian meal.

Jadi Butiyaan aur Mirch Masaale

Herbs, Spices and Flavourings

The most important aspect of Indian food is its flavour. The Indians use aromatic herbs and spices in their cooking in order to increase the flavour of food without masking the natural taste of the basic ingredients or their nutritive value. Most herbs and spices, if used in moderation, stimulate appetite and promote health; but the secret of their successful use is knowing their various combinations and proportions.

Spices should be stored in airtight containers, which should be kept in dry, dark, cool places. Wherever possible, spices should be ground freshly; they begin to lose their flavour if kept for long. Most spices are available in "whole" form so that they can be freshly ground; but if you have to buy spice powders, buy them in small quantities, making sure that they are fresh at the time of purchase.

It is interesting to note that it was the spices which attracted the first rush of Europeans to India; now there are a large number of Indians in Europe, as if to demonstrate how these spices should be used in making delicious food!

Given below is a list of the relatively more common and essential herbs, spices and flavourings; their Hindi names are given within brackets:

ANISEED (Patlee Saunf): A seed of the anise plant; an appetite stimulant used in wines, sweets and cordials; is claimed to prevent flatulence. It has a sweet smell and is served in Indian homes after a meal with *paans*, as a digestive.

ASAFOETIDA (Heeng): A strong digestive gum resin; it has a powerful smell and boasts medicinal properties. Often used to flavour *dhal* and vegetable preparations.

BAY LEAVES (Tej Patta): An aromatic herb with preservative and germicidal properties; used — either fresh or dried — for flavouring curried and dry dishes, but they are not eaten.

BLACK PEPPERCORNS (Gol Mirch): Rich in vitamin C; used to stimulate the heart and cure fevers. It is said to be the very first spice discovered by man; it is obtained from the berries of the pepper vine, which are dried by the sun into hard, black, brittle seeds. They are used whole or ground.

CAPSICUM *(Simla Mirch):* A large fleshy variety of pepper which is very mild in taste; also known as green pepper. Rich in vitamin C and served curried, chopped or stuffed.

CARDAMOM *(Illaichi):* They are of two types: brown *(bari)*, used extensively in Indian cookery in curries and *pullaos*; or *green (chhoti)*, — a fragrant and digestive spice, sold as green or whitish pods; used for flavouring many sweet and savoury dishes; also served with *paans.*

CAROM SEEDS *(Ajwain):* Also known as *thymol* seeds. A digestive and carminative spice, used in vegetable dry dishes and pickles. Cures coughs.

CAYENNE PEPPER *(Pisee laal mirch):* Obtained by grinding dried whole red chillies of the hottest ilk; "milder" red chillies, when ground, produce chilli powder. Use sparingly until sure of your level of acceptance.

CHILLIES *(Mirchen):* They can be fresh green *(hari)*, when they are even more pungent than red ones and add spicy flavour to food; or dry red *(laal)* when they are used whole or ground — the single hottest spice; use with care (see also cayenne).

CINNAMON *(Daalchini):* Used in stick or powdered form in curries, cakes and sweets; sticks are used only for flavouring and should not be eaten. A strong germicidal spice.

CLOVES *(Laung):* A powerful antiseptic. They are dried flower buds and are used whole or in powdered form in many sweets, savouries and spice powders.

CORIANDER *(Dhania):* Can be used as fresh green leaves *(hara)*, as seeds *(beej)* or as powder *(pisa)*. Coriander leaves are used for flavourings and garnishing and as an aromatic herb, similar to parsley. As whole seeds or in powdered form, coriander is a powerful carminative and is used in many spice mixtures, savouries, curries and pickles.

CUMIN SEEDS *(Zeera):* These are the seeds of a plant of the caraway family. The seeds can be white or black, but the former are the commonly used ones. Used whole or in powdered form for flavouring and preserving. A digestive spice.

CURRY LEAVES *(Meethi neem):* Aromatic leaves used extensively in South Indian main dishes and chutneys. Like bay leaves, they can be used fresh or dried and are added to dishes for flavouring.

FENNEL SEEDS *(Moti saunf):* These are plumper and milder cousins of the aniseed family. Used for flavouring, stuffing and pickles. Often served dry roasted as an after-dinner refresher.

FENUGREEK *(Methi):* Can be bought as green leaves *(saag)*, rich in vitamin C and as *bhaaji* is considered to be a great delicacy; or as seeds *(daana)*, rich in iron and used for flavouring curries or pickles. But use sparingly!

GARLIC *(Lahsun):* Garlic is a natural antibiotic blood cleanser and is rich in iron. It is a strong smelling bulb with segments known as cloves. Used in curries, chutneys, pickles and some side dishes; it is also available in powdered form.

GINGER, FRESH (Adrak): This light-brown gnarled root is used chopped, grated or ground in making curries, chutneys and dry dishes, and imparts to them a refreshing and pungent "kick". It has medicinal properties and is a carminative.

LOTUS PUFFS (Makhaane): These are lotus seeds; when they are roasted they puff up; used in many savoury and sweet dishes.

LOTUS STEMS (Bhasinda): Rich in vitamins and minerals, this is a cooking vegetable used for making kebabs, cutlets and side dishes.

MACE (Javitri): The outer membrane of nutmeg, sold as blades or powder. Used for flavouring curries and *pullaos*.

MINT (Podina): An aromatic herb used in *raitas* and chutneys; also used for garnishing.

MUSTARD SEEDS (Raai): Contain manganese and vitamin D; used for making pickles and dry dishes. These are tiny yellow or black seeds: highly nutritious and pungent in flavour, they have a tendency to dance around the pan and try to pop out when fried!

NIGELLA (Kalaunji): Little black onion seeds, normally used whole in pickles, stuffed vegetables and curries. Has a sophisticated flavour.

NUTMEG (Jaaiphal): A digestive agent, used for flavouring savouries and puddings; freshly ground nutmeg is preferable to the powdered form. Reduces flatulence.

ONION (Pyaaz): A flavouring and thickening agent used in curries and other side dishes. Young onions are known as spring onions (scallions *hari*) and taste lovely in chutneys and *raitas*. Contains vitamin D and sulphur.

SAFFRON (Kesar): The king of spices and perhaps the most expensive! Saffron strands are the dried stigmata of the saffron crocus which grows in abundance in Kashmir. Used for colouring and flavouring *pullaos* and puddings. Also available in powdered form.

SUGAR (Cheeni): Sugar is available in three basic varieties in Indian grocery stores. The refined white variety or *gur*, which is unrefined cane sugar, sold in big cakes. This has its own quality and taste. *Jaggery*, unrefined palm sugar, has a delicious and enjoyable flavour. Raw sugar, recommended for use in this book, is just normal sugar before its refinement!

TAMARIND (Imli): A seed pod used in its green or ripe form; it is first soaked in water and has its juice extracted. Adds piquancy to *chaat* and yogurt dishes and is made into sauces and chutneys.

TURMERIC (Haldi): A root spice which has a distinct yellow colour; sometimes used as a cheaper substitute for saffron. Used for its pungent flavour and for colouring *dhal*, curries, rice and many other side dishes. Good for the skin and has digestive properties.

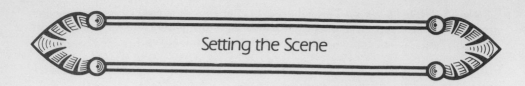

Setting the Scene

Traditionally, Indian meals are not served in courses as they are in the West or in other countries in Asia. All dishes are presented together at the outset on individual metal salvers (*thaalis*) containing several small metal bowls (*katoris*). Everyone eats sitting down. In large gatherings, it is customary for women to eat last; children being served first, followed by men. The beverage is ordinary tap water — not wine (actually, dry white wine or beer is perfectly acceptable with Indian food), but if you could afford champagne, perhaps we could compromise the tradition.

This scenario has changed in recent years. Indian homes now have western-style dining furniture, crockery and cutlery; buffet-style meals are not all that uncommon either. The current tendency is for the host to place the food centrally for the guests to help themselves. A good host always balances the menu — not only in terms of nutrition, but also from the point of view of texture and flavour. Make sure you offer a wide choice of dishes that complement each other and will appeal to lovers of the subtle flavours as well as the "fire eaters!" There is no hospitality to match that of an Indian host, whose every guest is an honoured one to be served the very choicest morsels.

If you are planning an Indian meal, you should create an Indian atmosphere. Play soft Indian music, burn fragrant incense and arrange fresh flowers. Make your dining table attractive by laying it with an Indian-style table cloth and arrange the napkins in glasses like flowers in a vase.

If your dining table is the main attraction, the dishes look appealing and the aroma of the food is tantalizing, even those who are not hungry will be tempted to sample your culinary creations. I offer a few suggestions which should help you achieve this. Serve your soups with croûtons; garnish curries and dry dishes with sliced tomato and green pepper and sprigs of coriander and fresh mint. Make serving dishes out of oranges and pineapples by scooping out their flesh and using the shells to serve *raitas* and sweet and sour dishes. When serving soft drinks, freeze some of the mixture in ice cube trays and serve the coloured cubes (which will add flavour, rather than dilute it) with the drinks. Decorate sweetmeats with edible silver and gold foil to give your dining room a festive and affluent look.

In addition to arranging food neatly and attractively, making it easy for guests to reach the dishes of their choice, as host it is your responsibility to arrange the food in the order in which it should be eaten — soup, or one of the other snacks; main dishes, such as curries, bread, rice and side dishes; sweet dishes, such as ice cream or *sharbat*; and finally, *paan* and its accompaniments.

I offer a few sample menus for your consideration.

1

a vegetarian soup
parauntha — layered or stuffed
a curry — possibly a *kofta*
two dry vegetables — one *bhaaji* and one stuffed
a pappadum — or fries
a *raita* or chutney
a sweetmeat
paan and accompaniments

2

a *pakora*
a *puri* or *kachauri*
a curry
a "whole" dish
a "stuffed" dish
a chutney and pappadum
a sweet dish or drink
paan and accompaniments

3

a *samosa*
a *chaat* dish
a *dosa* (or another South Indian dish)
accompanying sauces
a sumptuous sweetmeat or a *kulfi*
paan and accompaniments

4

golgappe
chapaatis
a *dhal* dish
2 dry vegetables
pappadums
a pickle and a chutney
a sweet
paan and accompaniments

5

a vegetarian soup
a rice *pullao* or *biriyaani*
a curry
a *raita*
fries or pappadums
a sweet or hot drink
paan and accompaniments

Chapter 1

Khaane ki Vishisht Cheezen
Remarkable Ingredients

The distinguished master chefs of India over the past centuries have developed ingredients which were until recently not altogether known in the West; similarly, the special Indian techniques of cooking — largely unknown beyond the shores of India — produce the exotic and delicious tastes inextricably connected with Indian food. It is these remarkable ingredients and methods which give Indian cuisine its enviable position and have put it on the highest pedestal of the world food league table.

The ingredients included in this section are usually made in advance for use in cooking later on; many are needed several times a day! Some of these are milk-based like *ghee* — the most popular, though expensive, medium of cooking in India; homemade cream cheese — used in making many sweets and savouries; and *khoya* — also used in sweets and savouries. Ground spices are the special assets of this section. Once you know the various spice mixtures, their differences and uses, you can get away from having to use commercial curry powder. You will then have the satisfaction of having prepared the real thing yourself!

These special concoctions are used in many different ways with the other, better-known cooking ingredients, and that unleashes a typically Indian culinary chemistry, which in turn produces amazing aromas and titillating tastes in Indian dishes.

Recipes for some of these remarkable ingredients are given in the following pages.

GHEE

Clarified Butter

Preparation time   5 minutes plus 30 minutes cooling time
Cooking time   30 minutes
Makes   4 cups

Ghee is the traditional medium for sautéeing or frying Indian food. It comes in two basic varieties: pure *ghee*, which is expensive but which leads to better-tasting dishes, and vegetarian *ghee*, made from vegetable shortening, which is cheaper but still makes tasty dishes. Make your own at home and be sure of what you have got!

Imperial (Metric)	American
2½ lb (1.15kg) unsalted butter	5 cups unsalted butter

1

Place the butter in a heavy-based saucepan over moderate heat. Bring to a boil, stirring all the time.

2

Lower heat, and simmer for 20 minutes until moisture has evaporated. With a wooden spatula, skim froth from top from time to time. Remove pan from heat, and let cool about 30 minutes.

3

Carefully strain the contents into a covered container, discarding residue at the bottom of the pan.

4

It will set as it cools; keep it covered, and take out the ghee to melt and use when required.

GHARELU DAHI

Homemade Yogurt

Preparation time   10 minutes plus setting time (5-24 hours)
Cooking time   20 minutes
Makes   2½ cups

Dahi is an important and versatile ingredient of the Indian kitchen; it is used in preparing many a curry, sweet drink or for making the cooling *raita* dishes.

Imperial (Metric)	American
1½ pints (900ml) creamy milk	3¾ cups half and half or milk
3 tablespoonsful natural yogurt	3 tablespoons plain yogurt

1

Boil the creamy milk (half and half) once. Alternatively, thicken ordinary milk by boiling 4 or 5 times.

2

Remove the pan from the heat, and let the milk cool a few minutes so that it is warm, but not hot. If milk is too hot, *dahi* will not set properly.

3

Beat the yogurt into milk. Then take another pan and pour the milk from one to the other, several times, in quick succession.

4

Transfer milk to a bowl, wrap bowl with a warm cloth, and allow to set in a warm place.

5

Normally the setting process will take about 24 hours; if the house is heated, the *dahi* might set in around 10 hours. In hot weather and if the bowl is placed in a cupboard, the *dahi* could set within 5 hours.

6

When set, use yogurt as needed.

CHHENA AUR PANEER

Homemade Cream Cheese

Preparation time	15 minutes plus 2 hours setting time
Cooking time	10 minutes
Makes	about 1 cup

Many mouth-watering Bengali sweetmeats are *chhena* based; when the *chhena* is flattened, pressed and set, it is christened *paneer* and is used for making several sizzling curries and savoury delights.

Imperial (Metric)	American
2 pints (1.15 litres) creamy milk	5 cups half and half or milk
3 tablespoonsful lemon juice	3 tablespoons lemon juice

1

Boil creamy milk (half and half) once. Alternatively, boil ordinary milk 3 or 4 times to thicken it.

2

When the milk has boiled, remove pan from heat and gradually add lemon juice; keep stirring until milk curdles. Let sit a few minutes.

3

Pour curdled milk through a muslin cloth and squeeze out whey. The remainder in the cloth is known as *chhena*; it should weigh around 8 ounces.

4

For use as *chhena* keep in the bowl, and use as needed for the dish you are making.

5

If, however, you require *paneer*, mould the *chhena* into a block, and press it under a heavy board or other heavy object. It will set and harden in about 2 hours.

6

Cut into desired shapes, and use for making savoury dishes.

KHOYA

Cooked Milk Concentrate

Preparation time	*5 minutes*
Cooking time	*40 minutes*
Makes	*½ cup*

Khoya is also known as *khoa* and *mawa*; it is used in making many Indian desserts and sweets. *Khoya* can be either plain or granulated; the recipe given here is for the latter variety, which is used to make stunning confections and also some curries. To make plain *khoya*, omit the lemon juice.

Imperial (Metric)	American
1 pint (600ml) creamy milk	2½ cups half and half or milk
1 teaspoonsful lemon juice	1 teaspoon lemon juice

1

Try to use creamy milk (half and half), or the net result will weigh less.

2

Place milk in a heavy-based (and if possible, non-stick) saucepan, and bring to a boil over high heat.

3

Stir in lemon juice so that milk curdles. Reduce heat to a simmer, and continue cooking.

4

Keep stirring so that milk does not stick to the base of the pan; as the milk thickens, stir even more vigorously. Use of a non-stick pan will save you some work, although occasional stirring will still be required.

5

When milk is reduced to a thick, dry lump the consistency of creamy pastry and stops sizzling, your stylish, granular *khoya* is ready.

6

Remove pan from heat, transfer *khoya* to a bowl, mould it into a circle and let cool; use as needed.

Note: Leftover *khoya* can be stored in the refrigerator for a few days.

GARAM MASALA

Ground Spice Mixture

Preparation time	10 minutes
Cooking time	10 minutes
Storage time	3 months

A curious phenomenon of Indian cooking is that each chef has his or her own recipe for *garam masala*; some have more than one! The spice powder is obtained by grinding a selection of spices — either by dry roasting them first, or not. *Garam masala* is the life and soul of all the major savoury dishes in an Indian meal. It is best to make your own at home.

Imperial (Metric)	*American*
1 oz (25g) white cumin seeds	3 tablespoons white cumin seeds
1 oz (25g) cloves	3 tablespoons cloves
1 oz (25g) coriander seeds	¼ cup coriander seeds
1 oz (25g) black peppercorns	¼ cup black peppercorns
4 bay leaves	4 bay leaves
1 (2-inch/5cm) cinnamon stick	1 (2-inch) cinnamon stick
4 brown cardamom pods	4 brown cardamom pods

1

Heat a griddle (or a heavy frying pan) over moderate heat and dry roast all the above ingredients about 10 minutes, stirring constantly.

2

When the spices give off a strong aromatic smell, remove from heat and grind by hand or in an electric grinder.

3

Strain powder through a muslin cloth and store in an airtight container.

4

Use when needed, closing the lid tightly after each use.

SAAMBHAR MASALA

Saambhar Powder

Preparation time   10 minutes
Cooking time   10 minutes
Storage time   about 3 months

This powder has a similar story to that of *garam masala*; the recipes for it vary. It is made like *garam masala* and can be stored for the same period. It is mainly used in making the vegetable sauce normally served with *dosa* and other South Indian dishes. Like most recipes included in this section, this one also saves a lot of eleventh-hour work!

Imperial (Metric)	American
10 dried curry leaves, crushed	10 dried curry leaves, crushed
5 tablespoonsful coriander seeds	⅓ cup coriander seeds
1 tablespoonful black peppercorns	1 tablespoon black peppercorns
Large pinch of asafoetida powder	Large pinch of asafoetida powder
10 dry red chillies, whole	10 dried red chili peppers, whole
3 tablespoonsful mixed dried	3 tablespoons mixed, dried beans
beans (pigeon peas, black beans	(pigeon peas, black beans and
and mung beans, crushed)	mung beans, crushed)
1 tablespoonful white cumin seeds	1 tablespoon white cumin seeds
1 teaspoonful fenugreek seeds	1 teaspoon fenugreek seeds
1 tablespoonful turmeric	1 tablespoon turmeric
1 tablespoonful mustard seeds	1 tablespoon mustard seeds

1

Heat a griddle (or a heavy-bottomed frying pan) over moderate heat and dry roast all the above ingredients for about 10 minutes.

2

When spices give off a strong aromatic smell, remove from heat and coarsely grind — either by hand or in an electric grinder (some prefer the mixture ground finely, in which case strain through a fine sieve before storing).

3

Store in an airtight container, and use as needed. Close the lid tightly after each use.

URAD KI WADI

Dried Black Bean Drops

Preparation time   35 minutes plus drying time
Storage time   3-6 months

These *wadis* are made and stored in advance, then cooked when the unexpected guest arrives, or when you want to prepare something different for a change. Many variations are possible.

Imperial (Metric)	American
1 lb (450g) skinless split black beans	2 cups skinless, split black beans
1 oz (25g) coriander seeds	¼ cup coriander seeds
1 oz (25g) white cumin seeds	3 tablespoons white cumin seeds
2 brown cardamom pods	2 brown cardamom pods
2 bay leaves	2 bay leaves
4 cloves	4 cloves
1 teaspoonful sea salt	1 teaspoon sea salt
8 dry red chillies, whole	8 dried red chili peppers, whole
10 black peppercorns	10 black peppercorns
Pinch of asafoetida powder	Pinch of asafoetida powder
8 oz (225g) pumpkin, chopped	1 cup pumpkin, chopped
Water as necessary	Water as necessary

1

Soak beans in water to cover overnight. Drain off water and grind beans not too finely.

2

Coarsely grind (by hand or in an electric grinder) all the spices.

3

Mix ground spices with ground beans. Add pumpkin, and adding water as necessary, whisk thoroughly into a thickish paste. Note that the more it is whisked, the better the *wadis* will be.

4

Spread out a clean cloth (the size of a bedspread) in the sun, or in the warmest place in the house, and drop 1 tablespoon paste on it, and at a distance of about 2 inches (5cm) another one; continue until paste is used up. Leave *wadis* to dry.

5

When moisture is gone and *wadis* are fully dry, pick them up from the cloth and store in an airtight container or plastic bag. Use as needed.

MUNGORI (MOONG WADI)

Dried Mung Bean Drops

Preparation time   40 minutes plus drying time
Storage time   3 months

These are like *urad dhal wadis* but are smaller in size, lighter on the stomach and have a slightly different taste. They are also made and stored in advance and cooked when needed. Similar preparations can be made with split peas and other pulses too.

Imperial (Metric)	American
1 lb (450g) skinless split mung beans	2 cups skinless, split mung beans
1 tablespoonful coriander seeds	1 tablespoon coriander seeds
1 tablespoonful white cumin seeds	1 tablespoon white cumin seeds
½ teaspoonful cayenne pepper	½ teaspoon cayenne pepper
4 peppercorns	4 peppercorns
Pinch of asafoetida powder	Pinch of asafoetida powder
1 teaspoon sea salt	1 teaspoon sea salt
Milk as necessary	Milk as necessary

1

Wash and soak the mung beans in enough water to cover overnight. Drain off water and grind the beans finely.

2

Grind all the spices into a fine powder by hand or in an electric grinder.

3

Add spice powder to ground beans and adding milk as necessary, whisk into a medium-thick paste. Whisk thoroughly for good results.

4

Take a large piece of clean cloth, spread it out in the sun or in the warmest place in the house, and drop half teaspoons of the mixture all over the cloth, about 1 inch (2.5cm) apart.

5

When moisture is all gone and *mungoris* are fully dry, pick them up from the cloth and store in a suitable airtight container or plastic bag.

6

Use as needed, replacing the lid tightly after each use.

TAYYAAR SHORWA

Ready Gravy

Preparation time	*10 minutes*
Cooking time	*2 minutes*
Makes	*2½ cups*

This gravy can be cooked in advance and reheated when needed. It is handy for adding to the *wadi, mungori* and *kofta* dishes. You may also use this preparation for most dry dishes.

Imperial (Metric)	American
8 oz (225g) ghee	1 cup ghee
2 large onions, finely chopped	2 large onions, chopped fine
4 large cloves garlic, sliced	4 large cloves garlic, sliced
1 teaspoonful grated fresh root ginger	1 teaspoon grated, fresh ginger root
2 teaspoonsful turmeric	2 teaspoons turmeric
2 teaspoonsful cayenne pepper	2 teaspoons cayenne pepper
2 teaspoonsful garam masala	2 teaspoons garam masala
4 ripe tomatoes, quartered	4 ripe tomatoes, quartered
5 tablespoonsful natural yogurt	⅓ cup plain yogurt
Sea salt, to taste	Sea salt, to taste
1 pint (600ml) tepid water	2½ cups tepid water

1

Heat the ghee in a deep saucepan over moderate heat, and sauté onions and garlic until golden. Stir in ginger, turmeric, cayenne pepper and garam masala — one by one — and stir-fry about 5 minutes.

2

Add tomatoes and yogurt; stir in salt and cook for 2 minutes.

3

Pour in water and bring to a boil. Reduce heat and simmer for about 10 minutes.

4

The gravy is now ready to use as needed.

TALE TUKRE

Crispy Croûtons

Preparation time   10 minutes
Cooking time   10 minutes
Makes   20 servings

Croûtons, or sippets, are fried cubes of bread; they add style and a decorative touch when served with soups and salads and will easily last a few days.

Imperial (Metric)	*American*
6 thick slices of wholemeal bread	6 thick slices whole wheat bread
Ghee for deep-frying	Ghee for deep frying

1
Remove the crusts from the bread and cut into small cubes.

2
Heat enough ghee in a *kadhai* or a deep frying pan to almost smoking point.

3
Lower heat and deep-fry the bread cubes — a few at a time — until golden all over, about 5 minutes. When cooked, remove from pan and drain on paper towels.

4
When completely dry and cool, store croûtons in an airtight container. Use as needed, but do not leave them out in the open for too long.

CHAASHNI

Sugar Syrup

Preparation time	5 minutes
Cooking time	20 minutes

Sugar syrup is used in the preparation of many Indian sweets; it can be made in many different strengths according to what is needed. This basic recipe is the vehicle through which many Indian sweets attain juicy and delectable heights!

Imperial (Metric)	American
1½ lb (675g) raw cane sugar	1½ pounds raw sugar
1½ pints (900ml) water	3¾ cups water
4 tablespoonsful milk	¼ cup milk

1

Place sugar and water in a deep saucepan, put over moderate heat and bring to a boil. Lower heat, and continue cooking.

2

Add half the milk to the cooking mixture; it will speedily bring the foam to the top. Remove and discard foam, using a wooden spatula. Then add remaining milk and clear foam again.

3

The syrup should now be clear and ready for use in most sweets. At this stage the syrup should be "1-string," i.e., when pressed between thumb and forefinger, a drop of syrup lifts up in one string; it takes about 15 minutes to reach this stage.

4

Continue cooking in order to obtain a 2-, 3- or 4-string syrup, until eventually it will crack into chips and convert into *misree* (Indian sugar candy).

Chapter 2

Garam Peya
Soups and Hot Drinks

Hot drinks are a valuable component of the survival kit during the freezing winter months. Soups are one variety of hot drink served at any time of the day or night. In India soups are served, by tradition, as light meals in themselves and have been drunk as such for centuries. The soups served in India today are British only in concept; they are still Indian in content. The first modern Indian soups were made in the South where the British were concentrated in the early days of the Raj. These soups were vegetarian; other variations came later.

Coffee in the South and tea in the rest of India are the staple hot drinks of the populace. Both these drinks are symbols of civilization and sophistication in the world today; India exports tons of tea and coffee to the West every year.

The Indian hot drink repertoire includes many drinks made from milk. Indians drink cow's milk (and other liquids made from it) with great reverence and relish.

Within the limited space available in this book, a selection of drinks from the various categories is offered here; I hope you find them enjoyable.

CHUKANDER AUR BHUTTE KA SOOP

Parsnip and Corn Soup

Serves	6
Preparation time	*15 minutes*
Cooking time	*30 minutes*

This is a classic soup dish which should please your friends and family alike.

Imperial (Metric)	American
8 oz (225g) parsnips, peeled and chopped	1½ cups parsnips, pared and chopped
8 oz (225g) fresh corn from the cob	1⅓ cups fresh corn from the cob
1½ pints (900ml) milk	3¾ cups milk
1 tablespoonful ghee	1 tablespoon ghee
1 small onion, finely chopped	1 small onion, finely chopped
2 green cardamom pods	2 green cardamom pods
½ pint (300ml) vegetable stock	1¼ cups vegetable stock
Sea salt and freshly ground black pepper, to taste	Sea salt and freshly ground black pepper, to taste
5 tablespoonsful fresh single cream	⅓ cup fresh, light cream
Pinch of grated nutmeg	Pinch of grated nutmeg

1

Place parsnip and corn in a deep saucepan and add the milk. Put over medium heat and bring to a boil. Let cool and purée in a blender.

2

In a separate saucepan, heat ghee and sauté onion and cardamom until golden. Pour in purée, add stock, season, and bring to a boil again.

3

Serve hot, topped with cream and nutmeg. (Or garnish soup with croûtons instead.)

SANTARE AUR PAALAK KA SOOP

Orange and Spinach Soup

Serves 4
Preparation time 10 minutes
Cooking time 25 minutes

This soup is rich in vitamins and iron and is good for the digestion.

Imperial (Metric)	American
1 large juicy orange	1 large, juicy orange
8 oz (225g) fresh spinach	4 cups fresh spinach
1 pint (600ml) water	2½ cups water
1 tablespoonful ghee	1 tablespoon ghee
1 small onion, peeled and chopped	1 small onion, peeled and chopped
Sea salt and freshly ground black pepper, to taste	Sea salt and freshly ground black pepper, to taste
½ pint (300ml) vegetable stock	1 cup vegetable stock
3 tablespoonsful fresh single cream, whipped	3 tablespoons fresh, light cream, whipped

1

Remove orange rind, grate it, and save for later garnishing. Remove pips and chop the orange. Trim, wash and chop the spinach.

2

Place chopped orange and spinach in a deep saucepan. Add measured water, place pan over medium heat, and cook until spinach is soft — about 10 minutes. Remove pan from heat and rub contents through a sieve.

3

Heat ghee in a separate saucepan and sauté onion until golden. Pour in sieved orange and spinach and stir in salt and pepper. Add stock, blend and bring to a boil. Simmer for about 10 minutes.

4

Serve hot topped with whipped cream and garnished with grated orange rind.

BUNDGOBHI KA SOOP

Cabbage Soup

Serves	*4*
Preparation time	*10 minutes*
Cooking time	*25 minutes*

This light dish is a veritable powerhouse of nourishment! I hope that everyone will like it.

Imperial (Metric)	American
8 oz (225g) white cabbage	½ pound white cabbage
4 spring onions	4 scallions
4 tablespoonsful ghee	4 tablespoons ghee
1 pint (600ml) water	2½ cups water
½ pint (300ml) vegetable stock	1¼ cups vegetable stock
2 ripe tomatoes, chopped	2 ripe tomatoes, chopped
Sea salt and freshly ground	Sea salt and freshly ground
black pepper	black pepper
Croûtons to garnish	Croûtons to garnish

1

Roughly chop the cabbage and spring onions (scallions).

2

Heat ghee in a deep saucepan and sauté cabbage and onion about 5 minutes, stirring all the time. Reserve some of the mixture for later garnishing; then add water, stock and tomatoes and bring to a boil. Continue cooking over medium heat until tender — about 15 minutes.

3

Remove pan from heat and mash contents into the liquid. Rub through a sieve, add seasoning to liquid and bring to a boil again.

4

Serve piping hot, garnished with croûtons and the reserved vegetable mixture.

SOOP PYAAZI

Onion Soup

Serves	6
Preparation time	10 minutes
Cooking time	25 minutes

This superb appetizer is known to ward off colds and will warm the cockles of your heart!

Imperial (Metric)	American
1 tablespoonful ghee	1 tablespoon ghee
3 large onions, peeled and chopped	3 large onions, peeled and chopped
2 slices wholemeal bread, chopped	2 slices whole wheat bread, chopped
½ pint (300ml) vegetable stock	1¼ cups vegetable stock
1 pint (600ml) milk	2½ cups milk
Sea salt and freshly ground black pepper	Sea salt and freshly ground black pepper
4 tablespoonsful fresh single cream	¼ cup light cream
Pinch of grated nutmeg	Pinch of grated nutmeg

1

Heat the ghee in a saucepan. Add onion, cover the pan, and cook gently until tender, stirring from time to time.

2

Drop in bread, stir in stock and cook a few minutes before adding milk. Bring to a boil; season and cook a little more — a total of about 20 minutes.

3

Remove pan from heat and serve hot. Add cream and sprinkle nutmeg on each serving.

MEWA KA SOOP

Nutty Soup

Serves	6
Preparation time	10 minutes
Cooking time	30 minutes

This dish has nutritional value and pleases the eye!

Imperial (Metric)	American
2 oz (50g) each: cashews, almonds and walnuts	¼ cup each: cashews, almonds and walnuts
2 tablespoonsful ghee	2 tablespoons ghee
1½ pints (900ml) creamy milk	3¾ cups milk or half and half
1 tablespoonful chopped onion	1 tablespoon chopped onion
½ pint (300ml) vegetable stock	1¼ cups vegetable stock
Pinch of grated nutmeg	Pinch of grated nutmeg
Sea salt and freshly ground black pepper, to taste	Sea salt and freshly ground black pepper, to taste
3 tablespoonsful finely chopped coriander leaves	3 tablespoons finely chopped cilantro (coriander)

1

Coarsely grind the nuts. Reserve some, sauté in ghee, and save for later garnishing.

2

Place the rest of the nuts in a saucepan; add milk and bring to a boil. Remove from heat and rub mixture through a sieve.

3

In a separate saucepan, heat ghee and sauté the onion. Then add sieved nut mixture and stock and cook over medium heat another 10 minutes. Stir in nutmeg and seasoning.

4

Serve hot, garnished with sautéed nuts and sprinkled with chopped coriander leaves.

MASOOR AUR CHANE KA SOOP

Lentil and Chick Pea Soup

Serves 4	
Preparation time 10 minutes plus overnight soaking	
Cooking time 30 minutes	

This soup is an exotic powerhouse in protein and sheer pleasure!

Imperial (Metric)	*American*
8 oz (225g) mixed lentils and chick peas, pre-soaked	1¼ cups mixed lentils and chick peas, presoaked
1 pint (600ml) water	2½ cups water
2 teaspoonsful ghee	2 teaspoons ghee
1 teaspoonful white cumin seeds	1 teaspoon white cumin seeds
Pinch of asafoetida powder	Pinch of asafoetida powder
½ pint (300ml) vegetable stock	1¼ cups vegetable stock
Sea salt and black pepper, to taste	Sea salt and black pepper, to taste
Juice of 1 lemon	Juice of 1 lemon
1 tablespoonful finely chopped coriander leaves	1 tablespoon finely chopped cilantro (coriander)

1

Place the lentils and chick peas in a deep saucepan and add the water. Put over medium heat and bring to a boil. Remove from heat. When cool, rub contents through a sieve.

2

Heat ghee in a separate saucepan and sauté cumin seeds and asafoetida for about 2 minutes. Add sieved liquid and stock; stir in salt and pepper and bring mixture to a boil.

3

Serve piping hot, sprinkled with lemon juice and chopped coriander leaves.

KAHWA MALAAIDAAR

Coffee with Cream

Serves	6
Preparation time	5 minutes
Cooking time	25 minutes

East and West are brought closer together by this creamy concoction.

Imperial (Metric)	American
5 tablespoonsful freshly ground coffee beans	⅓ cup freshly ground coffee beans
1½ pints (900ml) water	3¾ cups water
2 green cardamom pods	2 green cardamom pods
Raw cane sugar, to taste	Raw sugar, to taste
5 tablespoonsful double cream, whipped	⅓ cup heavy cream, whipped

1

Place the coffee in a bowl, and add a little water to make a paste. Transfer to a saucepan, adding the rest of the water. Boil for about 20 minutes.

2

Add cardamom and sugar; blend thoroughly, and cook for another 2 minutes.

3

Strain and serve piping hot, topped with whipped cream.

PODINA KI CHAAY

Mint Tea

Serves	4
Preparation time	5 minutes
Cooking time	15 minutes

This exotic hot drink invigorates all parts of your body!

Imperial (Metric)	American
1½ pints (900ml) water	3¾ cups water
16 fresh mint leaves	16 fresh mint leaves
2 teaspoonsful green tea leaves	2 teaspoons green tea leaves
¼ pint milk	⅔ cup milk
Raw cane sugar, to taste	Raw sugar, to taste

1

Place the water in a deep saucepan and bring to a boil.

2

Keeping pan on heat, add mint and tea; cover pan and cook for another minute.

3

Add milk and remove saucepan from heat.

4

Strain and serve hot, adding sugar as desired.

SAUNFI CHAAY

Fennel Tea

Serves 6
Preparation time   5 minutes
Cooking time   25 minutes

Good for inner warmth. Why not delight your family with this exotic beverage?

Imperial (Metric)	American
2 pints (1.15 litre) water	5 cups water
3 tablespoonsful fennel seeds	3 tablespoons fennel seeds
2 green cardamom pods	2 green cardamon pods
2 tea bags	2 tea bags
5 tablespoonsful fresh single cream	⅓ cup light cream
Raw cane sugar, to taste	Raw sugar, to taste

1

Place water in a deep saucepan and bring to a boil. Add fennel seeds and cardamom; cover and cook for another 5 minutes.

2

Still keeping pan on heat, drop in tea bags, cover and cook another minute.

3

Strain and serve hot, topped with cream, adding sugar as desired.

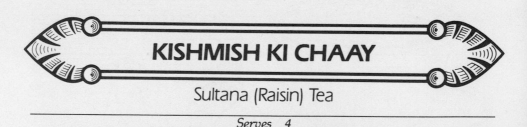

KISHMISH KI CHAAY

Sultana (Raisin) Tea

Serves 4
Preparation time   10 minutes
Cooking time   20 minutes

A rather unusual hot beverage which calls for a cultivated taste.

Imperial (Metric)	American
1½ pints (900ml) water	3¾ cups water
4 oz (100g) sultanas, cleaned and halved	⅔ cup golden seedless raisins, cleaned and halved
2 tea bags	2 tea bags
Raw cane sugar, to taste	Raw sugar, to taste
5 fl oz (150ml) soured cream	⅔ cup sour cream

1

Place the water and sultanas (golden seedless raisins) in a saucepan and bring to a boil over medium heat.

2

Add tea bags, cover pan and cook 2 more minutes.

3

Strain, stir in sugar and serve topped with sour cream.

POORVI CHAAY

Tea from the Orient

Serves 4	
Preparation time 5 minutes	
Cooking time 20 minutes	

A refreshing hot drink from the East, enjoyed equally in the West!

Imperial (Metric)	American
1½ pints (900ml) water	3¾ cups water
4 teaspoonsful Darjeeling tea leaves	4 teaspoons Darjeeling tea leaves
Raw cane sugar to taste	Raw sugar to taste
4 fresh lemon slices	4 lemon slices

1

Place the water in a saucepan and bring to a boil over medium heat.

2

Add tea and cook another 2 minutes. Stir in sugar and let dissolve.

3

Strain and serve scalding hot with a lemon slice floating on top of each serving.

CHAAY SANTARE WAALI

Orange Tea

Serves 6
Preparation time 5 minutes
Cooking time 20 minutes

An exotic novelty for tea drinkers.

Imperial (Metric)	American
2 pints (1.15 litres) water	5 cups water
2 green cardamom pods	2 green cardamom pods
1 juicy orange	1 juicy orange
6 tea bags	6 tea bags
Raw cane sugar, to taste	Raw sugar, to taste
4 tablespoonsful fresh single cream	¼ cup light cream

1

Place the water and cardamom in a deep saucepan and bring to a boil.

2

While water is heating, chop up the orange (including rind) and remove pips. When water boils, add orange and tea bags. Cover pan and continue to cook another 2 minutes or so.

3

Strain and serve steaming hot. Add cream and sugar to taste.

SHAAHI CHAAY

Royal Tea

Serves 6	
Preparation time 5 minutes	
Cooking time 25 minutes	

This beverage could quickly emerge as the hot favourite of royalty and commoners alike!

Imperial (Metric)	American
1 pint (600ml) water	2½ cups water
3 tablespoonsful tea leaves	3 tablespoons tea leaves
1 pint (600ml) Jersey milk	2½ cups milk or half and half
Raw cane sugar, to taste	Raw sugar, to taste
Pinch of ground cardamom	Pinch of ground cardamom
Whipped double cream, to serve	Whipped heavy cream, to serve

1

Place the water in a saucepan and bring to a boil. Add tea, cover pan and continue to cook another 2 minutes.

2

Boil milk in a separate saucepan. Stir in sugar and cardamom and, when sugar is dissolved, transfer contents to the other saucepan. Leave on heat for another minute to infuse.

3

Strain and serve boiling hot, topped with whipped cream.

DOODH BADAAM

Nutty Milk

Serves   4
Preparation time   5 minutes
Cooking time   25 minutes

Milk is a necessity for the sustenance of the human body. It can be served in various forms, and this preparation is a delicious one.

Imperial (Metric)	American
1½ pints (900ml) milk	3¾ cups milk
4 tablespoonsful raw cane sugar	4 tablespoons raw sugar
24 blanched, flaked almonds	24 blanched, slivered almonds
12 pistachios, sliced	12 pistachio nuts, sliced
1 tablespoonful sultanas, halved	1 tablespoon golden seedless raisins, halved
½ teaspoonful ground cardamom	½ teaspoon ground cardamom

1

Place the milk and sugar in a saucepan over medium heat and boil it twice.

2

Lower heat, add almonds, pistachios and sultanas (golden seedless raisins) and continue to cook another 15 minutes.

3

Serve hot, sprinkled with cardamom.

Chapter 3

Puri, Parauntha aur Paapad
Indian Bread Dishes

The varieties of Indian bread are legion! At least half of India's population eats bread of one kind or another at every meal; most of the other half eats it occasionally. Bread is generally made from wheat flour, but it is made from the flour of other grains as well.

Bread eaters in India are concentrated in Kashmir and the Punjab in the North; Gujrat, Goa and Maharashtra in the West; and Delhi and Uttar Pradesh in the Central area. Indian breads can, in the main, be placed into three categories: deep-fried, shallow-fried and dry fried. Deep-fried breads include the *puris* and *kachauris*; *paraunthas*, which are shallow-fried, can be plain, layered or stuffed in a variety of ways. Dry breads include the legendary *chapaati* or *phulka*; these can be stuffed, too. Some examples of each variety are offered here.

In the bread-eating areas, bread is the cornerstone of every main meal. Indian breads are generally eaten with one's fingers; normally only one hand is used for eating, the other being kept free for drinking water.

Chillas, or pancakes, are another variety of bread, often served on their own. Pappadums and fries also belong to the bread family; they are light and crunchy dishes, prepared in advance and cooked just before they are about to be served. I have included some representative samples of these dishes in this section and one recipe which describes an easy way to deep-fry the pappadums.

PHULKA

Basic Indian Bread

Serves   6
Preparation time   15 minutes plus 30 minutes resting time
Cooking time   25 minutes

This dry-cooked basic Indian bread is also called *chapaati* or *roti*. It is made in many sizes and many thicknesses; the Muslim families make paper-thin *rotis* which are wrapped in cloths and have to be folded up to 4 times before they can be accommodated on a normal plate or *thaali*. This dish is an integral part of a main meal and the mainstay of a vegetarian menu.

Imperial (Metric)	American
Pinch of sea salt	Pinch of sea salt
12 oz (350g) wholemeal flour	3 cups whole wheat flour
Water, as necessary	Water, as necessary
3 tablespoonsful flour, for dredging	3 tablespoons flour, for dredging
Ghee, to serve	Ghee, to serve

1

Mix the salt into the flour and place in a deep bowl. Add water as necessary and knead into a soft, pliable dough. Let rest about 30 minutes, covered with a damp cloth.

2

Knead dough thoroughly again; divide it into 12 portions and form into round balls. Using a board and rolling pin and dredging each ball generously in flour, flatten and roll out into thin, round discs.

3

Heat a griddle over medium heat until very hot. Cook each disc on the griddle about half a minute on each side; then place directly on heat and cook on both sides until it puffs up like a balloon. Make all *phulkas* in the same fashion.

4

Brush a little ghee on top of each *phulka* and serve hot, one at a time, as each is cooked.

METHI KI ROTI

Fenugreek Bread

Serves	4
Preparation time	15 minutes
Cooking time	20 minutes

This is a delicious and wholesome variety of Indian bread. However, those with frail digestive systems should eat it sparingly as it can be heavy on the stomach.

Imperial (Metric)	American
8 oz (225g) fenugreek leaves	4 cups fenugreek leaves
8 oz (225g) chick pea flour	2 cups chick pea flour
Pinch of sea salt	Pinch of sea salt
Pinch of cayenne pepper	Pinch of cayenne pepper
Pinch of garam masala	Pinch of garam masala
Water, as necessary	Water, as necessary
Ghee, to serve	Ghee, to serve

1

Clean and wash the fenugreek, then chop fine.

2

Place chick pea flour in a bowl. Add fenugreek, salt, cayenne pepper and garam masala. Adding water as necessary, make a medium-soft, pliable dough.

3

Divide dough into 8 portions and form into round balls. Roll each one out into a thin, round disc. Cover with a damp cloth.

4

Heat a griddle and cook discs one by one; first on the griddle and then exposed to direct heat. The discs should puff up when cooked.

5

Brush some ghee on the surface of each *roti* and serve hot one at a time, as soon as each is cooked.

BAAJRE KI ROTI

Millet Bread

Serves	*4*
Preparation time	*10 minutes*
Cooking time	*15 minutes*

This is a big, hefty *roti* which requires a cultivated taste. Serve with *dhal* and a leafy vegetable. If you like denser breads, increase the flour a little.

Imperial (Metric)	American
8 oz (225g) millet flour	2 cups millet flour
Milk, as necessary	Milk, as necessary
Ghee, to serve	Ghee, to serve

1

Place the flour in a deep bowl; make a well in the centre and add milk as necessary to make a dough of flaky consistency.

2

Divide dough into 4 portions and form into round balls. Wet palms, take one ball, flatten it, and then slap it from the palm of one hand to the other until you have a reasonable-sized thick, round disc.

3

Heat a griddle over medium heat and brush the surface with ¼ teaspoon ghee. Place disc on griddle. Turn it over after about one minute and cook on the other side. Then remove *roti* from griddle and place directly on heat for a few seconds on each side. This *roti* does not normally puff up.

4

Brush the desired amount of ghee on the surface and serve the *roti* hot, as soon as each is cooked.

TAGDI ROTI

Plain Stuffed Bread

Serves	6
Preparation time	15 minutes
Cooking time	25 minutes

Lads and lasses with healthy appetites and strong digestive systems will love this bread after a hard morning's work. Serve it with a robust *dhal* dish like *chana* or *rajmah*.

Imperial (Metric)	American
8 oz (225g) wholemeal flour	2 cups whole wheat flour
Water, as necessary	Water, as necessary
4 oz (100g) black bean powder	1 cup black bean powder
Pinch of asafoetida powder	Pinch of asafoetida powder
1 teaspoonful garam masala	1 teaspoon garam masala
1 clove garlic, crushed	1 clove garlic, crushed
½ teaspoonful sea salt	½ teaspoon sea salt
Ghee, to serve	Ghee, to serve

1

Place the flour in a bowl. Make a well in the centre, add sufficient water, and knead into a medium-soft dough. Divide dough into 12 portions and form into small round discs.

2

Place black bean powder in another bowl. Add asafoetida, garam masala, garlic, salt and enough water to bind ingredients into a smooth stuffing. Divide stuffing into 12 portions.

3

Take one dough disc, place a portion of stuffing on it and roll it up into a ball. Repeat with remaining dough and stuffing. Roll out each ball into a thin, round disc.

4

Heat a griddle and dry roast each disc on both sides; then expose each in turn to direct heat for a few seconds.

5

Brush a little ghee on the surface and serve hot.

PURI

Deep-Fried Bread

Serves	6
Preparation time	10 minutes
Cooking time	20 minutes

This is the most sophisticated of Indian breads; it is served on formal or special occasions. *Puris* are always smaller than *rotis* or *paraunthas*.

Imperial (Metric)	American
12 oz (350g) wholemeal flour	3 cups whole wheat flour
½ teaspoonful sea salt	½ teaspoon sea salt
Ghee, as necessary	Ghee, as necessary
Water, as necessary	Water, as necessary
3 tablespoonsful flour, for dredging	3 tablespoons flour, for dredging

1

Rub the flour and salt together with 2 teaspoons ghee. Add water as necessary to make a stiff dough.

2

Divide dough into 12 portions (18 if you want small *puris*); roll each one out into a thin, round disc. Cover with a damp cloth while the *kadhai* is being organized.

3

Heat sufficient ghee in a *kadhai,* or a deep frying pan, to smoking point. Slide in 2 discs at a time and deep-fry until brown on both sides. A *puri* takes no more than a minute to cook. When the *puris* are done, remove, and place on paper towels. Serve hot.

Note: Puris may also be served cold, in which case store them in an airtight container; they will then remain soft.

SINGHAARE KI PURI

Water Chestnut Flour Bread

Serves 4
Preparation time 10 minutes
Cooking time 20 minutes

These *puris* are delicious and can also be made with potatoes. For this preparation, the *puris* should be cooked as soon as the dough is ready; the dough should not be left to stand for any length of time.

Imperial (Metric)	American
Ghee, as necessary	Ghee, as necessary
8 oz (225g) water chestnut flour	2 cups water chestnut flour
8 oz (225g) yams (arbi), boiled, peeled and mashed	1 cup yams, boiled, peeled, and mashed
Pinch of asafoetida powder	Pinch of asafoetida powder
1 teaspoonful carom seeds	1 teaspoon carom seeds
2 green chillies, crushed	2 green chili peppers, crushed
½ teaspoonful sea salt	½ teaspoon sea salt

1

Rub 1 tablespoon ghee into the flour and add the yams together with the rest of the ingredients. Knead thoroughly to form a stiff dough (water will not normally be required for this dough).

2

Divide dough in 12 portions, and make small balls of each. Using a greased board and a rolling pin, roll each one out into a thickish, round disc.

3

Heat sufficient ghee in a *kadhai*, or a deep frying pan, and deep-fry these discs — about 4 at a time — over moderate heat until they are light brown on both sides.

4

Drain, and serve straight from the *kadhai*, with a curry or a dry vegetable preparation.

MOONG KACHAURI

Mung Bean Bread

Serves 6
Preparation time   20 minutes plus overnight soaking and 20 minutes resting time
Cooking time   30 minutes

The stuffed variety of deep-fried breads is a connoisseur's delight! Stuffings can be varied to suit personal tastes — any of the *dhals* or vegetables can be substituted to prepare the filling.

Imperial (Metric)	American
8 tablespoonsful dried mung beans	½ cup dried mung beans
8 oz (225g) wholemeal flour	2 cups whole wheat flour
Water, as necessary	Water, as necessary
Ghee, as necessary	Ghee, as necessary
1 teaspoonful white cumin seeds	1 teaspoon white cumin seeds
Large pinch of sea salt	Large pinch of sea salt
Pinch of cayenne pepper	Pinch of cayenne pepper
½ teaspoonful garam masala	½ teaspoon garam masala
½ teaspoonful green mango powder	½ teaspoon green mango powder

1

Wash the mung beans and soak in water overnight. Then rinse and drain off water and grind beans coarsely.

2

Sift the flour into a deep bowl, and rub in 2 teaspoons ghee. Gradually add enough water, and knead into a stiff but pliable dough. Divide dough into 12 portions, and form into small, fat discs. Cover with a damp cloth, and let dough rest about 20 minutes while stuffing is being prepared.

3

Heat 1 tablespoon ghee, and sauté cumin until it changes colour, then stir in ground beans together with the rest of the ingredients. Cook about 5 minutes over medium heat, stirring constantly. When moisture has evaporated, remove from heat and let cool. Divide stuffing mixture into 12 portions.

4

Take one disc of dough, smear surface with ghee and place one portion of stuffing on it. Roll it up and roll out into a thick, small round. Make the remaining rounds similarly.

5

Heat sufficient ghee in a *kadhai* or a deep frying pan, and deep-fry the rounds (*kachauris*) about 2 at a time — over low heat until they are golden on both sides.

6

Drain on paper towels and serve hot.

CHAAWAL KI PURI

Boiled Rice Bread

Serves   6
Preparation time   15 minutes
Cooking time   25 minutes

This *puri* is an all-rounder and can be served with a main meal, as a snack or with drinks — it is delicious whichever way you serve it! You may use left-over boiled rice, too.

Imperial (Metric)	*American*
4 oz (100g) cooked brown rice	½ cup cooked brown rice
3 oz (75g) wholemeal flour	¾ cup whole wheat flour
3 oz (75g) chick pea flour	¾ cup chick pea flour
1 tablespoonful natural yogurt	1 tablespoon plain yogurt
½ teaspoonful sea salt	½ teaspoon sea salt
Pinch of freshly ground black pepper	Pinch of freshly ground black pepper
Ghee, as necessary	Ghee as necessary

1

Place the rice in a large bowl; add the flours and yogurt, and knead.

2

Add a little ghee as necessary (but no water), stir in salt and pepper, and knead thoroughly into a stiff, yet pliable, dough.

3

Divide dough in 12 portions; roll each one out, with a bread board and rolling pin, into a thin, round disc.

4

Heat sufficient ghee in a *kadhai*, or a deep frying pan, and deep-fry these discs — 2 to 3 at a time — until golden brown on both sides.

5

When cooked, remove and drain on paper towels; serve hot if possible.

ALOO PARAUNTHA

Potato-Stuffed Bread

Serves 4

Preparation time 15 minutes plus 30 minutes resting time

Cooking time 25 minutes

This dish is a good example of stuffed shallow-fried bread and should prove popular.
Serve it with a curry and yogurt dish.

Imperial (Metric)	American
8 oz (225g) wholemeal flour	2 cups whole wheat flour
Water, as necessary	Water, as necessary
2 medium-sized potatoes, boiled,	2 medium-sized potatoes, boiled,
peeled and mashed	peeled and mashed
½ teaspoonful sea salt	½ teaspoon sea salt
½ teaspoonful green mango powde	½ teaspoon green mango powder
½ teaspoonful garam masala	½ teaspoon garam masala
1 green chilli, finely chopped	1 green chili pepper, finely chopped
1 tablespoonful chopped	1 tablespoon chopped
coriander leaves	cilantro (coriander)
Ghee, as necessary	Ghee, as necessary

1

Place the flour in a bowl; make a well in the centre, add water as necessary and
knead into a medium-soft dough. Let stand for 30 minutes.

2

While dough is resting, mix remaining ingredients together, except for *ghee*. When
well blended, divide stuffing into 8 portions.

3

Divide the dough into 8 portions. Roll out each portion into a thin, round disc.

4

Place one portion of stuffing on a disc of dough, roll it up into a ball, then roll it out
— using a bread board and rolling pin — into a thickish, round disc. Make all 8
discs; handle them carefully.

5

Heat a griddle until very hot, and grease its surface with 1 teaspoon ghee. Place disc
on griddle, applying some ghee on the surface of the disc. After about 30 seconds,
turn disc over and cook on the other side. Keep turning it over and applying a little
more ghee each time, until *parauntha* is done and little brown spots appear on both
sides. Serve hot, straight from the griddle.

PARATI PARAUNTHA

Layered Bread

Serves 4
Preparation time   15 minutes plus 20 minutes resting time
Cooking time   15 minutes

Paraunthas are made in many ways; this particular dish is very tasty, wholesome and filling. It can be served at virtually any meal, day or night. In the Punjab these *paraunthas* are served at breakfast.

Imperial (Metric)	American
Large pinch of sea salt	Large pinch of sea salt
1 lb (450g) wholemeal flour	4 cups whole wheat flour
Ghee, as necessary	Ghee, as necessary
Tepid water, as necessary	Tepid water, as necessary

1

Sift the salt and flour into a deep bowl and rub in 1 tablespoon ghee. Adding tepid water as necessary, knead into a medium-stiff but pliable dough. Cover with a damp cloth and let rest for about 20 minutes.

2

Knead again and divide the dough into 8 portions. Roll each portion into a ball; flatten on a floured surface and roll out into a thick disc. Apply a thick layer of ghee to the surface and fold disc in half; grease surface again, and fold in half again, to give you a triangular shape. Flatten this triangle with a floured rolling pin. Make similar triangles from the remaining portions.

3

Heat a griddle over medium heat until very hot. Brush griddle with ½ teaspoon ghee, and slap *parauntha* onto it. Now brush the top of the triangle generously with ghee. Turn over after a minute, lower heat, and cook *parauntha* for a minute on the other side. When dark brown spots appear on each side, the *parauntha* is ready.

4

Serve hot, straight from the griddle.

MOOLI PARAUNTHA

Radish Bread

Serves 4
Preparation time 15 minutes plus 30 minutes resting time
Cooking time 20 minutes

This is a scrumptious delicacy of the *parauntha* clan; fillings can be changed according to personal preferences. It can be served on its own, or with a curry and a pickle.

Imperial (Metric)	American
8 oz (225g) wholemeal flour	2 cups whole wheat flour
Water, as necessary	Water, as necessary
5 tablespoonsful grated white	5 tablespoons grated
radish (*mooli*)	white radish
Large pinch of sea salt	Large pinch of sea salt
1 tablespoonful grated onion	1 tablespoon grated onion
1 green chilli, finely chopped	1 green chili pepper, finely chopped
Pinch of grated, fresh ginger root	Pinch of grated, fresh ginger root
½ teaspoonful green mango powder	½ teaspoon green mango powder
Ghee, as necessary	Ghee, as necessary

1

Sift the flour into a deep bowl. Gradually add water and knead into a medium-pliable dough. Cover with a damp cloth, and let rest about 30 minutes.

2

Make the stuffing by first squeezing the water from the radish, then putting it in a bowl; add sea salt, onion, chilli, ginger and mango powder and blend thoroughly. Divide mixture into 8 portions.

3

Knead dough again and divide into 8 portions. Flatten and roll out each portion on a floured surface into a small, round disc. Brush a little ghee on the disc, place one portion of stuffing on it, and roll it up into a ball. Then flatten it with your hand and roll it out into a thin disc. Make remaining stuffed discs similarly.

4

Heat a griddle until very hot and shallow-fry each disc with ghee until dark brown spots appear on both sides.

5

When cooked, drain *paraunthas* on paper towels and serve hot.

MOONG KA CHILLA

Mung Bean Pancake

Serves   4

Preparation time   10 minutes plus overnight soaking

Cooking time   20 minutes

This is an unusual type of bread; nevertheless, it is commonly made in many areas of India and with several different ingredients. Serve with a yogurt dish or a favourite pickle.

Imperial (Metric)	American
8 oz (225g) dried mung beans	1 cup dried mung beans
Water, as necessary	Water, as necessary
Sea salt, to taste	Sea salt, to taste
1 green chilli, chopped	1 green chili pepper, chopped
Pinch of garam masala	Pinch of garam masala
1 teaspoonful shredded coriander leaves	1 teaspoon shredded cilantro (coriander)
Ghee, as necessary	Ghee, as necessary

1

Wash the mung beans thoroughly and soak in water overnight. Drain off water.

2

Grind beans finely over a *sil-batta* (or use an electric blender). Transfer to a deep bowl. Add water as necessary to make a thin batter of dropping consistency.

3

Stir salt, chilli, garam masala and coriander into batter and blend thoroughly.

4

Heat a griddle or frying pan; brush pan with ½ teaspoon ghee, and pour 1 tablespoon batter on it. Quickly spread the batter around pan. Baste with another ½ teaspoon ghee, and turn pancake (*chilla*) over. It is done when it is golden on both sides.

5

Serve one at a time, straight from the frying pan.

PAAPAD KI PAKAAI

The Cooking of Pappadums

Serves 6
Preparation time 5 minutes
Cooking time 5 minutes

The pappadum is a very lightweight dish and its making and cooking are specialities of Indian cuisine. Many Indian families have spent generations perfecting the art of pappadum manufacture. But I offer one or two recipes in this book so you can manufacture your own!

There are many varieties of pappadum: from paper thin to quite thick, and bland to blazing hot; they can be cooked in many ways too — baking in the oven, cooking under a grill (broiler) or deep-frying, the last being the most popular. You may serve them by themselves as snacks, or with a meal.

All pappadums can be cooked in the same way, irrespective of their ingredients.

Imperial (Metric)	American
3 pappadum rounds, quartered	3 pappadum rounds, quartered
Ghee, for deep-frying	Ghee, for deep-frying

1

Place enough ghee in a *kadhai*, or a deep frying pan, and heat nearly to smoking point.

2

When temperature is adequate (test by dropping a little piece of pappadum in the ghee; if it sizzles immediately, the ghee is ready), drop a piece of pappadum in the *kadhai*, from the side. Cook one at a time.

3

Soon after sliding the pappadum into the *kadhai*, press it with a spatula for a couple of seconds; then turn over and do the same on the other side. This enables the pappadum to spread to its fullest extent and prevents it from curling up.

4

It takes only seconds for the pappadum to cook on both sides. Remove when done, and drain on paper towels. Leave for several seconds to firm up.

5

Serve hot and crisp.

CHAAWAL PAAPAD

Brown Rice Pappadum

Serves 20 plus	
Preparation time	15 minutes plus drying time
Cooking time	30 minutes

This is a variety of pappadum you can make and store in advance, then cook when required. Pappadums are made in the shape of thin, round discs, but they can be broken into convenient pieces. Then they fry without curling up!

Imperial (Metric)	American
8 oz (225g) brown rice	1 cup brown rice
1 pint (600ml) water	2½ cups water
Pinch of baking powder	Pinch of baking powder
½ teaspoonful sea salt (or to taste)	½ teaspoon sea salt (or to taste)
Pinch of cayenne pepper	Pinch of cayenne pepper
Pinch of ground cumin	Pinch of ground cumin
Ghee, to grease	Ghee, to grease

1

Grind the rice into a powder.

2

Sift the rice powder into a bowl. Add water, baking powder, salt, cayenne pepper and cumin — one by one. Whisk thoroughly to make a batter.

3

Place batter in a lidded saucepan. Bring to a boil over medium heat. Lower the heat and continue cooking.

4

Invert lid, or take a metal plate, and grease its surface with a little ghee. Take out 1 tablespoon of the cooking mixture and spread it over the inverted lid. Then replace lid on pan. Soon the mixture on the lid will firm up into a disc. Remove it, and make the remainder similarly.

5

Grease a piece of plastic and place all the discs, as they come off the lid of the pan, to dry out in the sun or warmest place in the house. The discs will shrink as they dry.

6

When dry, store discs in a covered container, and deep-fry when required.

ALOO PAAPAD

Potato Pappadums

Serves   10 plus
Preparation time   15 minutes plus drying time
Cooking time   10 minutes

Ready-made pappadums are available from your grocer, but you can make this variety at home in advance and store them for later use. The seasoning in pappadums is added during preparation; so when the time comes, you just deep-fry and serve!

Imperial (Metric)	American
1 lb (450g) potatoes	1 pound potatoes
Pinch of baking powder	Pinch of baking powder
1 teaspoonful sea salt (or to taste)	1 teaspoon sea salt (or to taste)
½ teaspoonful chilli powder	½ teaspoon chili powder (or coarsely
(or coarsely ground black pepper)	ground black pepper)
Tepid water, as necessary	Tepid water, as necessary ,
Vegetable oil, to grease	Vegetable oil, to grease

1
Boil the potatoes; then peel and mash them.

2
Add the baking powder, salt and chilli powder to potato. Mix together to form a dough, adding tepid water as necessary. Divide the dough into 10 portions.

3
Make a thin round of each portion — by hand or by pressing it against a greased flat surface — then spread rounds on a greased plastic sheet either in the sun or warmest place in the house.

4
When rounds are completely dry on both sides, store in an airtight container and deep-fry when needed.

TARBOOZ KACHRI

Watermelon Rind Fries

Serves	*20 plus*
Preparation time	*10 minutes plus drying time*
Cooking time	*5 minutes*

An easily made crunchy snack. Prepare in advance and store; deep-fry just before use. These dishes are sprinkled with condiments at the time of serving.

Imperial (Metric)	American
1 small, ripe watermelon	1 small, ripe watermelon
Ghee or vegetable oil, to deep-fry	Ghee or vegetable oil, to deep-fry
Sea salt, to taste	Sea salt, to taste
Ground black pepper, as required	Ground black pepper, as required
Chilli powder, as necessary	Chili powder, as necessary

1

Cut the watermelon into thick slices. Remove the red flesh together with seeds and use them in another preparation.

2

Chop up the slices, consisting of the outer skin and a layer of white flesh, into small shreds. Squeeze out moisture, and put it out to dry — in the sun or the warmest place in the house.

3

When watermelon is completely dry, place in a suitable covered container.

4

Just before use, deep-fry the required quantity in ghee or vegetable oil and serve sprinkled with desired condiments.

KARELA KACHRI

Bitter Gourd Fries

Serves 10 plus	
Preparation time 10 minutes plus 2 hours resting and drying time	
Cooking time 5 minutes	

Make and store these in advance; that unexpected guest will never catch you unawares! Similar preparations can be made from many other fruits and vegetables.

Imperial (Metric)	American
1 lb (450g) bitter gourds	1 pound bitter gourds
1 tablespoonful sea salt	1 tablespoon sea salt
Vegetable oil, to deep-fry	Vegetable oil, to deep-fry
Preferred condiments	Preferred condiments

1

Wash the bitter gourds and shred them.

2

Place the bitter gourds in a large bowl and sprinkle with salt. Let rest at least 2 hours.

3

Wash shreds continuously for 5 minutes under a warm tap. Squeeze out water and put out to dry completely — either in the sun or the warmest place in the house.

4

Store in an airtight container to use when needed.

5

Deep-fry in oil just before use; sprinkle with condiments of your choice and serve freshly made.

Chapter 4

Chaawal
Rice

Brown rice is versatile and is more nutritious than the milled and polished white variety. It is rich in protein, minerals and vitamins; and all because of its brown husk and high fibre. The fibrous content of the rice expedites the digestive processes and purifies the blood; the vitamin-rich layers of bran prevent obesity in addition to satisfying the appetite. Brown rice is always palatable: Cook it properly and present it well; careful chewing can also enhance the flavour and pleasure derived from it.

Even though brown rice is nutty, flavoursome and delicious, it is not generally eaten in India. The reason could well be that people cannot get used to its texture. The only advice I can offer to remedy this is that you should try varying the proportion of water and the cooking times until you get the texture to your liking. Immediately, a whole new world of brown rice dishes appears on the horizon, whether or not you subscribe to the macrobiotic philosophy of eating!

Rice is now grown in all the continents and in diverse temperatures and climates. Like its white polished counterpart, brown rice also comes in short, medium and long grains; the grains range from $\frac{1}{4}$ to $\frac{1}{2}$ inch in length. Long-grain brown rice is the best for most Indian dishes as the grains, when cooked, are dry and do not stick to each other. Although this rice is more expensive than others, it is worth the extra expense!

Although many types of brown rice are available in the marketplace — red rice, wild rice, organic rice and sweet brown — the organically-grown variety is preferable. Such rice is grown under the most natural methods and is consequently strong and healthy. Chemical fertilizers — the bane of modern technology — are shunned under this system, and vegetable composts are used instead. The best quality organic rice is produced in northern Italy and on the West coast of the United States.

SAADE CHAAWAL

Plain Boiled Rice

Serves	4
Preparation time	20 minutes
Cooking time	30 minutes

This is one of the basic rice preparations. Always wash the rice in several changes of water and soak it for 20 minutes in warm water (or 30 minutes in cold water).

Imperial (Metric)	American
1 lb (450g) long grain brown rice, pre-soaked	2 cups long-grain brown rice, presoaked
1½ pints (900ml) water	3¾ cups water
1 tablespoonful butter	1 tablespoon butter

1

Place the rice and water in a deep saucepan with a heavy bottom; put over medium heat and bring to a boil — cook about 15 minutes.

2

Remove pan from heat and drain off any excess water; then return pan to very low heat. Cover pan, and cook another 10 minutes.

3

Take pan off heat. Remove lid, add butter and mix carefully with a fork (not a spoon). Then replace lid, and let rice rest about 5 minutes.

4

Serve hot.

PEELE CHAAWAL

Yellow Rice

Serves 4
Preparation time 20 minutes
Cooking time 25 minutes

This rice dish will bring colour not only to your dining table but to your cheeks also! Serve with a curry and/or a yogurt preparation.

Imperial (Metric)	American
3 tablespoonsful ghee	3 tablespoons ghee
1 medium-sized onion, chopped	1 medium-sized onion, chopped
½ teaspoonful turmeric	½ teaspoon turmeric
2 bay leaves	2 bay leaves
4 cloves	4 cloves
4 black peppercorns	4 black peppercorns
2 (1-inch/2.5cm) cinnamon sticks	2 (1-inch) cinnamon sticks
2 each: brown and green cardamom pods	2 each: brown and green cardamom pods
1 lb (450g) long grain brown rice, pre-soaked	2 cups long-grain brown rice, presoaked
1½ pints (900ml) water	¾ cups water
3 tablespoonsful fresh green peas	3 tablespoons fresh, green peas
1½ teaspoonsful sea salt (or to taste)	1½ teaspoons sea salt (or to taste)
Pinch of saffron	Pinch of saffron

1

Heat the ghee in a *kadhai*, or a deep frying pan, and sauté the onion over medium heat until golden. Reserve some onion for later garnishing.

2

Add turmeric to onion, and stir a few times. Then stir in the rest of the spices and mix well.

3

Add the rice and stir a few times. Then pour in water and bring to a boil.

4

Turn down the heat, mix in peas and salt, cover pan and cook another 10 to 15 minutes.

5

Sprinkle with saffron and the reserved sautéed onion and serve hot.

BHAGONE KE NAMKEEN CHAAWAL

Savoury Rice Casserole

Serves	4
Preparation time	15 minutes
Cooking time	20 minutes

Here is an exotic rice dish. Serve with a *raita* or curry for lunch.

Imperial (Metric)	American
3 tablespoonsful ghee	3 tablespoons ghee
1 teaspoonful white cumin seeds	1 teaspoon white cumin seeds
1 small onion, chopped	1 small onion, chopped
1 lb (450g) cooked long grain brown rice	2 cups cooked, long-grain brown rice
8 oz (225g) halved button mushrooms, lightly fried	3 cups halved button mushrooms, lightly sautéed
1 teaspoonful sea salt (or to taste)	1 teaspoon sea salt (or to taste)
½ teaspoonful freshly ground black pepper	½ teaspoon freshly ground black pepper
3 fl oz (90ml) hot vegetable stock	6 tablespoons hot vegetable stock
1 oz (25g) wholemeal breadcrumbs	½ cup whole wheat breadcrumbs
1 tablespoonful chopped coriander leaves	1 tablespoon chopped cilantro (coriander)

1

Heat the ghee in a frying pan and sauté the cumin and onion until golden.

2

Place the rice and mushrooms in an ovenproof casserole. Spoon ghee mixture over it. Add seasoning and stock.

3

Put casserole in a preheated oven 15 to 20 minutes until contents are well-blended.

4

Sprinkle with breadcrumbs and coriander (cilantro)and serve hot.

GARI KE CHAAWAL

Coconut Rice

Serves	4
Preparation time	20 minutes
Cooking time	35 minutes

This is a delicious rice preparation. Serve it with a main meal, to eat with a curry, pappadums and other side dishes.

Imperial (Metric)	American
3 tablespoonsful ghee	3 tablespoons ghee
1 teaspoonful white cumin seeds	1 teaspoon white cumin seeds
Pinch of turmeric	Pinch of turmeric
2 cloves	2 cloves
4 black peppercorns	4 black peppercorns
2 brown cardamom pods	2 brown cardamom pods
6 oz (175g) desiccated coconut	2 cups dried coconut
1 lb (450g) long grain brown rice, pre-soaked	2 cups long-grain brown rice, presoaked
1½ pints (900ml) water	3¾ cups water
1½ teaspoonsful sea salt (or to taste)	1½ teaspoons sea salt (or to taste)
1 tablespoonful chopped almonds, cashews and sultanas, lightly fried	1 tablespoon chopped almonds, cashews and golden seedless raisins, lightly sautéed

1

Heat the ghee in a heavy saucepan and sauté the cumin until golden brown. Add turmeric, cloves, peppercorns and cardamom and stir about a minute.

2

Stir in coconut and sauté until golden. Then add rice and continue sautéing, over medium heat, another 2 minutes.

3

Pour in water; add salt and bring to a boil. Lower heat, cover pan and continue cooking until rice is cooked and water has evaporated — about 20 minutes.

4

Sprinkle nuts and dried fruit over preparation and serve hot.

URAD KI KHICHDI

Rice and Black Beans

Serves	6
Preparation time	20 minutes
Cooking time	35 minutes

Traditionally, this preparation is quite moist when ready; however, you may drain off some water and have a *pullao*-like preparation. According to my family's firm belief, a *khichdi* has four "boyfriends": yogurt, pappadums, ghee and pickles!

Imperial (Metric)	American
1 lb (450g) brown rice, pre-soaked	2 cups brown rice, presoaked
8 oz (225g) split black beans, pre-soaked	1 cup split black beans, presoaked
2½ pints (1.5 litres) water	6¼ cups water
2 teaspoonsful sea salt (or to taste)	2 teaspoons sea salt (or to taste)
6 black peppercorns	6 black peppercorns
2 dry red chillies	2 dried, red chili peppers
½ teaspoonful turmeric	½ teaspoon turmeric
1 tablespoonful ghee	1 tablespoon ghee
Pinch of asafoetida powder	Pinch of asafoetida powder
1 teaspoonful white cumin seeds	1 teaspoon white cumin seeds

1

Place the rice and black beans in a heavy saucepan; add water together with salt, peppercorns, chillies and turmeric and bring to boil over medium heat — cook about 10 minutes.

2

Lower heat and simmer until rice and black beans are tender — about 20 minutes.

3

Heat ghee in a frying pan and sauté asafoetida and cumin about 2 minutes. When cumin seeds begin to pop, remove pan from heat.

4

Pour ghee mixture over *khichdi* and serve hot.

CHAAWAL METHI ALOO

Fenugreek and Potato with Rice

Serves 4	
Preparation time 20 minutes	
Cooking time 30 minutes	

This is a self-contained rice meal. Serve with a yogurt preparation or pickle and a pappadum. You may substitute spinach if fenugreek is not available.

Imperial (Metric)	American
3 tablespoonsful vegetable oil	3 tablespoons vegetable oil
1 teaspoonful white cumin seeds	1 teaspoon white cumin seeds
2 oz (50g) chopped onion	⅓ cup chopped onion
2 potatoes, diced	2 potatoes, diced
1 lb (450g) fenugreek leaves, chopped	1 pound fenugreek leaves, chopped
1 lb (450g) long grain brown rice, pre-soaked	2 cups long-grain brown rice, presoaked
1½ pints (900ml) water	3¾ cups water
2 teaspoonsful sea salt (or to taste)	2 teaspoons sea salt (or to taste)
1 green chilli, chopped	1 green chili pepper, chopped
1 teaspoonful garam masala	1 teaspoon garam masala

1

Heat the oil in a saucepan and sauté cumin and onion until golden.

2

Stir in the potato and fenugreek, cover pot and cook over medium heat about 5 minutes, stirring occasionally.

3

Add rice, pour in water together with salt and green chilli and bring to a boil; do not cover pan.

4

Reduce heat to low, cover pan and continue to cook another 10 minutes.

5

Sprinkle with garam masala 5 minutes before serving.

ALOO TAMAATAR PULLAO

Potato and Tomato Pullao

Serves	*4*
Preparation time	*20 minutes*
Cooking time	*35 minutes*

A fine and flavoursome *pullao*, sure to please that discerning guest!

Imperial (Metric)	American
4 small potatoes, scraped and sliced	4 small potatoes, scraped and sliced
Ghee, as necessary	Ghee, as necessary
1 tablespoonful chopped onion	1 tablespoon chopped onion
½ teaspoonful grated root ginger	½ teaspoon grated ginger root
2 bay leaves	2 bay leaves
2 brown cardamom pods	2 brown cardamom pods
4 cloves	4 cloves
1 lb (450g) long grain brown rice, pre-soaked	2 cups long-grain brown rice, presoaked
1½ pints (900ml) water	3¾ cups water
Sea salt and pepper, to taste	Sea salt and pepper, to taste
2 red tomatoes, quartered	2 red tomatoes, quartered
3 tablespoonsful fried cashews	3 tablespoons sautéed cashews

1

Sauté the potato in 2 teaspoons ghee in a saucepan. When golden, remove potato and put on a plate.

2

Add 1 tablespoon ghee to saucepan and sauté onion and ginger until golden. Stir in bay leaves, cardamom and cloves and sauté 2 more minutes.

3

Add potato and rice to the spices and stir thoroughly 2 minutes. Then pour in water, mix in seasoning and bring to a boil over medium heat.

4

Lower heat, cover pan and cook about 15 minutes. Add tomato and cook another 10 minutes or so until rice is tender and water has evaporated.

5

Serve hot, sprinkled with sautéed cashew nuts.

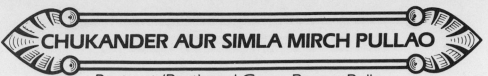

CHUKANDER AUR SIMLA MIRCH PULLAO

Beetroot (Beet) and Green Pepper Pullao

Serves	4
Preparation time	20 minutes
Cooking time	30 minutes

This is a splendid *pullao*. You may experiment with alternatives such as mushrooms and turnips. Serve with pappadums and a yogurt dish for lunch or dinner

Imperial (Metric)	American
3 tablespoonsful ghee	3 tablespoons ghee
1 onion, finely sliced	1 onion, finely sliced
2 bay leaves	2 bay leaves
2 brown cardamom pods	2 brown cardamom pods
1 teaspoonful mustard seeds	1 teaspoon mustard seeds
1 large beetroot, sliced	1 large beet, sliced
2 large green peppers, sliced	2 large green peppers, sliced
1 lb (450g) long grain brown rice, pre-soaked	2 cups long-grain brown rice, presoaked
1½ pints (900ml) water	3¾ cups water
Sea salt and pepper, to taste	Sea salt and pepper, to taste
1 tablespoonful lemon juice	1 tablespoon lemon juice
1 tablespoonful chopped coriander leaves	1 tablespoon chopped cilantro (coriander)

1

Heat the ghee in a saucepan and sauté the onion until golden. Add bay leaves, cardamom and mustard and sauté 2 to 3 minutes.

2

Stir in beetroot (beet) and green pepper and sauté another 2 minutes or so.

3

Add rice and water together with seasoning and bring to a boil — cook about 10 minutes.

4

Lower heat, sprinkle with lemon juice and coriander, cover pan and simmer another 10 to 15 minutes until rice is cooked and water has evaporated.

5

Serve hot.

BHUTTE KI BIRIYANI

Rice with Sweetcorn

Serves	*4*
Preparation time	*20 minutes*
Cooking time	*25 minutes*

This traditionally mild dish delights young and old alike; it is open to experimentation! Serve it with pappadums, pickles and yogurt concoctions.

Imperial (Metric)	*American*
5 tablespoonsful ghee	5 tablespoons ghee
3 tablespoonsful chopped onion	3 tablespoons chopped onion
2 cloves garlic, chopped	2 cloves garlic, chopped
2 bay leaves	2 bay leaves
Pinch of asafoetida powder	Pinch of asafoetida powder
½ teaspoonful turmeric	½ teaspoon turmeric
2 (½-inch/1.25cm) cinnamon sticks	2 (½-inch) cinnamon sticks
8 oz (225g) sweetcorn	1½ cups fresh corn kernels
1 lb (450g) cooked long grain brown rice	2 cups cooked, long-grain brown rice
Sea salt and black pepper, to taste	Sea salt and black pepper, to taste
½ teaspoonful garam masala	½ teaspoon garam masala
1 tablespoonful lemon juice	1 tablespoon lemon juice
3 tablespoonsful chopped coriander leaves	3 tablespoons chopped cilantro (coriander)

1

Heat the ghee in a heavy saucepan and sauté the onion and garlic until golden. Add spices and stir-fry, over medium heat, about 2 minutes.

2

Add sweetcorn, stir well and continue cooking until corn is almost tender — about 10 minutes.

3

Mix in rice and the seasoning; lower heat and cook another 5 minutes. Remove from heat, sprinkle garam masala over mixture, cover pan and let rest 5 minutes.

4

Add lemon juice and serve hot, garnished with coriander.

GOBHI KI BIRIYANI

Rice with Cauliflower

Serves	4
Preparation time	30 minutes
Cooking time	35 minutes

Here is another sophisticated rice dish for the connoisseur! Delight your friends and family with your brilliance in *biriyani*-making.

Imperial (Metric)	American
4 tablespoonsful ghee	4 tablespoons ghee
1½ teaspoonsful white cumin seeds	1½ teaspoons white cumin seeds
Pinch of asafoetida powder	Pinch of asafoetida powder
2 bay leaves	2 bay leaves
4 green cardamom pods	4 green cardamom pods
8 oz (225g) cauliflower florets	2¼ cups cauliflower florets
½ teaspoonful turmeric	½ teaspoon turmeric
2 teaspoonsful sea salt (or to taste)	2 teaspoons sea salt (or to taste)
½ teaspoonful freshly ground black pepper	½ teaspoon freshly ground black pepper
1 lb (450g) cooked long grain brown rice	2 cups cooked, long-grain brown rice
5 tablespoonsful natural yogurt	⅓ cup plain yogurt
Chopped coriander leaves, to garnish	Chopped cilantro (coriander), to garnish

1

Heat the ghee in a heavy saucepan and sauté cumin and asafoetida 2 minutes. Add bay leaves and cardamom; stir well.

2

Toss in cauliflower and sauté for 5 minutes over medium heat. Stir in turmeric and seasoning and cook another 10 minutes.

3

Add rice and yogurt; stir carefully, lower heat, cover pan and cook another 10 to 15 minutes.

4

Sprinkle with coriander and serve hot.

Chapter 5

Dhalen
Pulses and Legumes

Indian pulses (legumes) abound in protein; they are rich in vitamins, too. They can be cooked with or without their skins; whole or split; powdered or in paste form. Powdered pulses are often mixed with other ingredients to make delicacies absolutely out of this world! They are also cooked as fillings, purées or just plain *dhals*. They can be easily substituted for vegetable curries; equally, they can be doubled up with them, too! The large variety of pulses available in the marketplace can conjure up tremendous sensations of distinctive delights with fantastic flavours. Pulses have great food value, whatever you do with them.

A little secret for your ears! Dhal dishes do not easily go wrong; with a little imagination you can cook masterpieces which will please the palate and attract attention. A little skill in this field will do nothing but good for your reputation as an accomplished cook.

Pulses are an integral part of an "informal" vegetarian meal. They are economical to buy and simple to cook, and are sure to impress those who have broken the ethnic food barrier and have come to admire Indian food. Indian pulse preparations are not just a group of remarkable dishes, they are an institution!

ARHAR KI DHAL

Pigeon Peas

Serves 4

Preparation time 10 minutes plus 2 hours soaking time

Cooking time 40 minutes

This is one of the most popular *dhal* dishes, usually served with boiled rice or chapaatis. Rich in protein, pigeon peas can be prepared in many different ways and with many combinations of ingredients; this is one of them.

Imperial (Metric)	American
4 oz (100g) pigeon peas	½ cup pigeon peas
1 pint (600ml) water	2½ cups water
½ teaspoonful turmeric	½ teaspoon turmeric
1 green mango, peeled and sliced	1 green mango, peeled and sliced
Sea salt, to taste	Sea salt, to taste
3 tablespoonsful ghee	3 tablespoons ghee
1 teaspoonful white cumin seeds	1 teaspoon white cumin seeds
½ teaspoonful cayenne pepper	½ teaspoon cayenne pepper
1 tablespoonful chopped coriander leaves	1 tablespoon chopped cilantro (coriander)

1

Wash the pigeon peas and soak about 2 hours.

2

Place pigeon peas and water in a saucepan and bring to a boil over medium heat. Stir in turmeric, mango and sea salt and cook another 20 minutes, with the pan half covered.

3

Heat ghee in a frying pan and sauté cumin until it sizzles and changes colour; then stir in cayenne pepper.

4

Add ghee mixture to pigeon peas and cook another 5 to 10 minutes until the *dhal* is the desired consistency.

5

Serve hot, sprinkled with coriander.

RAAJMAH

Whole Kidney Beans

Serves 4

Preparation time 10 minutes plus overnight soaking

Cooking time 30 minutes

This dish, when ready, should be moist, but you may make the preparation thinner by adding more water. Serve as a substitute for, or in addition to, a basic *dhal*.

Imperial (Metric)	American
8 oz (225g) kidney beans	1¼ cups kidney beans
1 pint (600ml) water	2½ cups water
Sea salt, to taste	Sea salt, to taste
4 oz (100g) melted butter	½ cup melted butter
3 tablespoonsful chopped onion	3 tablespoons chopped onion
2 cloves garlic, chopped	2 cloves garlic, chopped
2 fresh green chillies, chopped	2 fresh green chili peppers, chopped
1 teaspoonful mustard seeds	1 teaspoon mustard seeds
1 teaspoonful garam masala	1 teaspoon garam masala
2 tablespoonsful chopped coriander leaves	2 tablespoons chopped cilantro (coriander)

1

Wash the beans and soak them overnight.

2

Place the beans and water in a deep saucepan, with a pinch of sea salt, and bring to a boil over medium heat — cook about 10 minutes.

3

Meanwhile in a *kadhai*, or another saucepan, heat butter and sauté onion and garlic until golden. Add chillies and mustard and sauté another 2 minutes.

4

Transfer beans (reserving the liquid for later) to the *kadhai* in which the butter and onion mixture is cooking. Cover and cook over medium heat another 5 minutes.

5

Add reserved cooking liquid with sea salt to taste; also stir in garam masala and continue cooking for 10 minutes.

6

Serve hot, sprinkled with coriander leaves.

DHULI MASOOR DHAL

Washed Lentils

Serves   4
Preparation time   10 minutes
Cooking time   40 minutes

Eating this *dhal* is an experience to cherish! Lentils occupy an exalted position in the line-up of legume preparations and can be used to make a whole range of delicacies.

Imperial (Metric)	American
8 oz (225g) lentils, washed and pre-soaked	1 cup lentils, washed and presoaked
1 pint (600ml) water	2½ cups water
Sea salt, to taste	Sea salt, to taste
2 cloves garlic, quartered	2 cloves garlic, quartered
1 green chilli, chopped	1 green chili pepper, chopped
1 teaspoonful mustard seeds	1 teaspoon mustard seeds
3 tablespoonsful ghee	3 tablespoons ghee
1 teaspoonful white cumin seeds	1 teaspoon white cumin seeds
Pinch of chilli powder	Pinch of chili powder

1

Place the lentils and the measured water in a saucepan, put over medium heat and bring to boil — cook about 10 minutes.

2

Stir in salt, garlic, green chilli and mustard; lower heat and simmer about 30 minutes, until *dhal* is soft.

3

Meanwhile take a frying pan and heat ghee to a very high temperature. Toss in cumin seeds and chilli powder.

4

Serve *dhal* hot, sprinkled with ghee mixture.

SAABUT URAD DHAL

Whole Black Beans

Serves 4

Preparation time   10 minutes plus overnight soaking

Cooking time   30 minutes

This preparation is rich in protein and forms part of an informal meal. Serve with a bread or rice.

Imperial (Metric)	American
4 oz (100g) whole black beans	½ cup whole black beans
1 pint (600ml) water	2½ cups water
1 (1-inch/2.5cm) piece fresh root ginger	1 (1-inch) piece fresh ginger root
2 cloves garlic, chopped	2 cloves garlic, chopped
Sea salt, to taste	Sea salt, to taste
2 tomatoes, chopped	2 tomatoes, chopped
Pinch of garam masala	Pinch of garam masala
2 oz (50g) ghee	4 tablespoons ghee
½ teaspoonful cayenne pepper	½ teaspoon cayenne pepper
Pinch of asafoetida powder	Pinch of asafoetida powder

1

Pick over and clean the beans; then wash and soak overnight.

2

Place the beans and the measured water in a heavy saucepan, or *batloi*, and bring to a boil.

3

Stir in ginger, garlic and salt; half-cover pan and cook about 20 minutes over medium heat.

4

Add tomato and garam masala and cook another 10 minutes.

5

Meanwhile, in a separate frying pan, heat ghee together with cayenne pepper and asafoetida for 2 minutes.

6

Serve beans hot, topped with a little ghee mixture on each serving.

MOONG SAAGWAALI

Dried Mung Beans with Spinach

Serves 4

Preparation time 10 minutes plus 2 hours soaking time

Cooking time 30 minutes

This dish is an interesting variation of the basic *dhal* dish, and can also be substituted for a vegetable curry. It is rich in protein and light on the stomach.

Imperial (Metric)	American
4 oz (100g) skinless mung beans	½ cup skinless mung beans
8 oz (225g) spinach, chopped	4 cups spinach, chopped
1½ pints (900ml) water	3¾ cups water
Sea salt, to taste	Sea salt, to taste
Pinch of turmeric	Pinch of turmeric
1 tablespoonful ghee	1 tablespoon ghee
1 tablespoonful chopped onion	1 tablespoon chopped onion
Pinch of chilli powder	Pinch of chili powder
1 teaspoonful white cumin seeds	1 teaspoon white cumin seeds

1

Wash the beans and soak about 2 hours.

2

Place the beans and spinach in a deep saucepan and cook over medium heat about 20 minutes.

3

Stir in sea salt and turmeric, cover pan, and let cook another 5 minutes.

4

Meanwhile, in a frying pan, heat ghee and sauté onion until golden. Then add chilli powder and cumin and sauté 2 minutes.

5

Mix ghee mixture with beans and spinach and cook another 5 minutes.

6

Serve hot, with a bread or rice.

CHANA AUR URAD KI DHAL

Split Peas and Black Beans

Serves 6

Preparation time   10 minutes plus 1 hour soaking time

Cooking time   40 minutes

This is a delicious *dhal* dish, a veritable powerhouse of protein! Serve with a main meal.

Imperial (Metric)	American
4 oz (100g) split peas	½ cup split peas
4 oz (100g) skinless dried black beans	½ cup skinless dried black beans
1½ pints (900ml) water	3¾ cups water
½ teaspoonful turmeric	½ teaspoon turmeric
2 teaspoonsful sea salt	2 teaspoons sea salt
3 tablespoonsful melted butter	3 tablespoons melted butter
¼ teaspoonful asafoetida powder	¼ teaspoon asafoetida powder
1 teaspoonful grain mustard	1 teaspoon grain mustard
1 green chilli, chopped	1 green chili pepper, chopped
1 tablespoonful chopped coriander leaves	1 tablespoon chopped cilantro (coriander)

1

Wash the split peas and beans in several changes of water, and soak at least 1 hour.

2

Place the measured water together with split peas and beans in a saucepan. Put it over medium heat and bring to a boil — cook for about 10 minutes.

3

Stir in turmeric and salt; lower heat, half-cover pan and simmer another 25 minutes or so until pulses (legumes) are tender.

4

Meanwhile, heat butter; add asafoetida, mustard and chilli and sauté, covered, about 2 minutes. When mustard starts spluttering around noisily, pour this mixture over *dhal* in saucepan.

5

Cover saucepan and continue cooking another 2 to 3 minutes. Serve hot, sprinkled with coriander.

PANCHRATNI DHAL

Mixed Pulses (Legumes)

Serves 6
Preparation time   10 minutes plus 2 hours soaking time
Cooking time   40 minutes

The consistency of this preparation can be thick or thin, as desired. If it is to be served with rice, it should be on the thin side. It offers a wide scope for experimentation any way it is prepared.

Imperial (Metric)	*American*
8 oz (225g) mixture of 5 pulses of your choice	1 cup mixture of 5 legumes of your choice
1½ pints (900ml) water	3¾ cups water
½ teaspoonful turmeric	½ teaspoon turmeric
Sea salt, to taste	Sea salt, to taste
2 oz (50g) melted butter	¼ cup melted butter
Pinch of asafoetida powder	Pinch of asafoetida powder
3 tablespoonsful chopped onion	3 tablespoons chopped onion
1 green chilli, chopped	1 green chili pepper, chopped

1

Wash the pulses (legumes) and soak in cold water about 2 hours.

2

Place the measured water in a deep saucepan and bring it to a boil over medium heat. Add pulses (legumes) and simmer 20 minutes.

3

Stir in turmeric and sea salt; lower heat, half-cover the pan and cook for another 10 minutes.

4

Meanwhile heat butter in a frying pan and sauté asafoetida and onion until brown at the edges. Add chilli and blend well.

5

Pour mixture over pulses (legumes) and serve hot.

Note: Leftover *dhal* preparations can be stored in the refrigerator to be reheated later; serve topped with a hot ghee and white cumin seed mixture.

PHARA

Bread and Pigeon Peas

Serves   6

Preparation time   10 minutes plus 2 hours soaking time

Cooking time   40 minutes

Although you can vary this *dhal*, this particular combination is not only tasty and flavoursome, it is a complete two-in-one meal. Serve by itself with a dry vegetable dish and a chutney.

Imperial (Metric)	American
8 oz (225g) pigeon peas	1 cup pigeon peas
2 pints (1.15 litres) water	5 cups water
1 teaspoonful turmeric	1 teaspoon turmeric
Sea salt, to taste	Sea salt, to taste
4 oz (100g) wholemeal flour	1 cup whole wheat flour
Water as necessary	Water as necessary
2 oz (50g) ghee	4 tablespoons ghee
1 tablespoonful white cumin seeds	1 tablespoon white cumin seeds
Large pinch of cayenne pepper	Large pinch of cayenne pepper
1 tablespoonful green mango powder	1 tablespoon green mango powder
3 tablespoonsful chopped coriander leaves	3 tablespoons chopped cilantro (coriander)

1

Wash the pigeon peas under running water and then soak 2 hours or so.

2

Place the measured water and pigeon peas in a deep saucepan; put over medium heat and bring to a boil. Stir in turmeric and salt, half-cover pan and continue cooking.

3

While *dhal* is cooking, knead flour with enough water to make it a soft dough; divide it into 12 portions and roll each one out into a thin, round disc.

4

When *dhal* has been on the heat about 30 minutes, slide dough discs into the saucepan — one by one — then cover pan and cook another 10 minutes.

5

Meanwhile heat ghee and sauté cumin until it changes colour. Then stir in cayenne pepper and blend. Pour this mixture over *dhal* concoction.
Sprinkle mango powder and coriander (cilantro) over preparation and serve hot.

MATAR KI DHAL AUR LAUKI

Split Peas and Marrow (Squash)

Serves 4	
Preparation time 10 minutes plus 2 hours soaking time	
Cooking time 40 minutes	

This is a delightful dish; serve with bread or boiled rice. If you prefer, chick peas and cucumber can be substituted for the main ingredients.

Imperial (Metric)	American
4 oz (100g) dried split peas	1 cup dried split peas
1 pint (600ml) water	2½ cups water
4 oz (100g) marrow, grated	1 scant cup summer squash, grated
½ teaspoon turmeric	½ teaspoon turmeric
Sea salt, to taste	Sea salt, to taste
½ green mango, sliced	½ green mango, sliced
1 tablespoon ghee	1 tablespoon ghee
1 tablespoon chopped onion	1 tablespoon chopped onion
1 green chilli, chopped	1 green chili pepper, chopped

1

Wash the split peas and soak about 2 hours.

2

Place water in a saucepan and bring it to a boil; add peas, and cook over medium heat about 15 minutes.

3

Add marrow (squash), turmeric, salt and mango; lower heat, cover pan and cook another 15 minutes or so until peas are tender.

4

Meanwhile, heat ghee in a frying pan and sauté onion until golden. Stir in chilli and cook for another minute or so; then pour over *dhal* mixture.

5

Serve hot.

MASOOR AUR TORAI

Lentils with Courgettes (Zucchini)

Serves	4
Preparation time	10 minutes
Cooking time	35 minutes

This is an exotic and unusual *dhal* concoction. Experts sing psalms to the flavour and looks of lentils on their own; with courgettes (zucchini), the preparation becomes even better!

Imperial (Metric)	American
4 oz (100g) lentils	½ cup lentils
1 pint (600ml) water	2½ cups water
½ teaspoonful turmeric	½ teaspoon turmeric
3 tablespoonsful vegetable oil	3 tablespoons vegetable oil
1 tablespoonful chopped onion	1 tablespoon chopped onion
2 cloves garlic, chopped	2 cloves garlic, chopped
1 (½-inch/1.25cm) piece of root ginger, sliced	1 (½-inch) piece ginger root, sliced
1 green chilli, chopped	1 green chili pepper, chopped
1 small courgette, cut into convenient pieces	1 small zucchini, cut into convenient pieces
Sea salt, to taste	Sea salt, to taste
½ teaspoonful garam masala	½ teaspoon garam masala
1 teaspoonful white cumin seeds	1 teaspoon white cumin seeds

1

Place the lentils, water and turmeric in a saucepan over medium heat and bring to a boil. Continue cooking, removing the froth from the top from time to time.

2

In a separate saucepan, heat half the oil and sauté onion and garlic until golden. Then stir in ginger, chilli and courgette (zucchini) and mix thoroughly. Cook over medium heat about 5 minutes.

3

Transfer lentils to the pan with courgette (zucchini) mixture. Stir in sea salt and garam masala; half-cover pan, lower heat and cook another 15 minutes.

4

In remaining oil, sauté cumin over medium heat until it sizzles and changes colour.

5

Serve lentils hot, topped with cumin mixture.

DHANSAK

Pulses (Legumes) with Vegetables

Serves 4
Preparation time   10 minutes plus 1 hour soaking time
Cooking time   40 minutes

Dhansak is a speciality of the Indians of Persian extraction who worship fire and are known as the Parsees. The word means a wealthy pedigree, i.e., a dish of high style and quality. *Dhansak* can be both vegetarian or non-vegetarian — this dish is of the vegetarian ilk; among the vegetables you may include the leafy variety.

Imperial (Metric)	American
8 oz (225g) mixed pulses	1 cup mixed legumes
of your choice	of your choice
1½ pints (900ml) water	3¾ cups water
1 lb (450g) mixed vegetables, cut into	1 pound mixed vegetables, cut into
convenient pieces	convenient pieces
4 tablespoonsful ghee	4 tablespoons ghee
1 small onion, chopped	1 small onion, chopped
2 cloves garlic, chopped	2 cloves garlic, chopped
1 green chilli, chopped	1 green chili pepper, chopped
½ teaspoonful turmeric	½ teaspoon turmeric
2 teaspoonsful garam masala	2 teaspoons garam masala
Sea salt, to taste	Sea salt, to taste
1 tablespoonful lemon juice	1 tablespoon lemon juice
3 tablespoonsful chopped	3 tablespoons chopped
coriander leaves	cilantro (coriander)

1

Wash the pulses (legumes) in several changes of running water and soak at least 1 hour.

2

Place the water and pulses (legumes) in a saucepan; put over medium heat and bring to a boil. Add vegetables and cook another 10 minutes.

3

Heat the ghee in another deep saucepan and sauté the onion and garlic until golden; then stir in chilli, turmeric and garam masala and mix thoroughly.

4

Transfer *dhal* and vegetable mixture into pan with ghee and spices; stir in sea salt, cover pan and cook a further 20 minutes or so until pulses (legumes) and vegetables are tender. Add lemon juice and coriander (cilantro) and serve hot.

Chapter 6

Shorwedaar Sabziyaan
Curries

Indian curries are a legend; they are the most famous of Indian dishes. However, it is wrong to imagine that all Indian food can be described in the one word "curry". Curry is the name given to a group of dishes which have gravy in them — some are thin and watery, others are moist. Curries are made in many, many ways, resulting in a spectrum of tastes and appearances.

Every region in India specializes in making its own variety of curries. Generally, they start with mild ones in the North; by the time you reach the South, they become hot and fiery. The ingredients used in making these curries are those grown locally — and there is truly a bewildering variety of vegetables and other ingredients used in making these dishes.

Whichever way curries are made, some spices are used in all of them. Whether used whole or in powdered form, nearly all spices contain nutritional or medicinal properties. Contrary to some people's belief, spices are food for good health and do not harm your mental or physical faculties. It must be realized, however, that excessive use of spices will be harmful; first you must determine your normal level of acceptance and stick with it; then you may decrease or increase the quantities of spices to obtain "milder" or "hotter" curries. In absolute terms, it is impossible to define what is a "mild" or "hot" curry: the "mild" curries of the South are "hotter" than the "hot" curries of the North!

I hope you will find my selection of recipes for this section tasty and enjoyable.

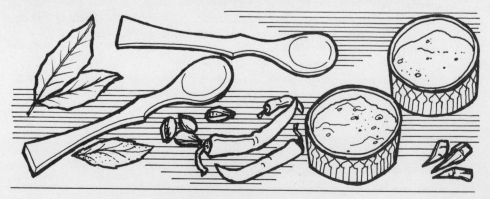

ALOO MATAR RASEDAAR

Potato and Pea Curry

Serves 4
Preparation time 10 minutes
Cooking time 25 minutes

A simple and economical vegetarian curry — do offer it to your friends and family to curry favour with them!

Imperial (Metric)	American
5 tablespoonsful ghee	5 tablespoons ghee
1 medium-sized onion, chopped	1 medium-sized onion, chopped
2 cloves garlic, chopped	2 cloves garlic, chopped
2 cloves	2 cloves
2 bay leaves	2 bay leaves
1 (1-inch/2.5cm) cinnamon stick	1 (1-inch) cinnamon stick
1 teaspoonful garam masala	1 teaspoon garam masala
1 teaspoonful chilli powder	1 teaspoon chili powder
½ teaspoonful turmeric	½ teaspoon turmeric
½ teaspoonful ground coriander	½ teaspoon ground coriander
2 tomatoes, quartered	2 tomatoes, quartered
Sea salt, to taste	Sea salt, to taste
1 tablespoonful natural yogurt	1 tablespoon plain yogurt
2 medium potatoes, cut into	2 medium potatoes, cut into
small pieces	small pieces
3 oz (75g) green peas	½ cup green peas
½ pint (300ml) warm water	1¼ cups warm water
Chopped coriander leaves, to garnish	Chopped cilantro (coriander), to garnish

1

Heat the ghee in a saucepan and sauté the onion and garlic over medium heat until golden. Add cloves, bay leaves and cinnamon and stir-fry another 2 minutes.

2

Add garam masala, chilli powder, turmeric, coriander, tomatoes, salt and yogurt and mix well. Add potatoes and peas; pour in water and bring to a boil.

3

Lower heat, cover pan and simmer gently about 15 minutes, or until vegetables are done.

4

Garnish with coriander leaves (cilantro) and serve hot.

ARBI CHUKANDER SHORWEDAAR

Curried Yams and Beetroot (Beets)

Serves   4

Preparation time   15 minutes plus marinating time

Cooking time   40 minutes

If you are looking for an exotic and colourful curry, this is it. The amount of liquid can be adjusted, just as other vegetables can be substituted if desired.

Imperial (Metric)	*American*
8 oz (225g) yams (arbi)	1 medium yam (arbi)
Sea salt, to taste	Sea salt, to taste
3 tablespoonsful natural yogurt	3 tablespoons plain yogurt
4 oz (100g) ghee	½ cup ghee
1 tablespoonful chopped onion	1 tablespoon chopped onion
1 clove garlic, sliced	1 clove garlic, sliced
2 bay leaves	2 bay leaves
1 (1-inch/2.5cm) cinnamon stick	1 (1-inch) cinnamon stick
½ teaspoonful cayenne pepper	½ teaspoon cayenne pepper
8 oz (225g) beetroot, peeled and sliced	1¼ cups beets, peeled and sliced
½ pint (300ml) ready gravy (page 28)	1¼ cups ready gravy (page 28)
1 teaspoonful garam masala	1 teaspoon garam masala

1

Scrape yams; prick with a fork (without breaking them), sprinkle 2 teaspoons salt over them and smear with yogurt. Let marinate 30 minutes.

2

Heat half the ghee and sauté yams over medium heat for 5 minutes. Then remove from pan and reserve.

3

Return pan to the heat and add remaining ghee. Sauté the onion and garlic until transparent. Add bay leaves, cinnamon and cayenne pepper, and stir a couple of minutes. Add beetroot (beets) and stir-fry about 5 minutes.

4

Reheat gravy in a separate saucepan. Then add yams and the contents from the other pan. Cover pan, lower heat and cook about 20 minutes.

5

Just before serving, sprinkle garam masala over the preparation and remove from heat.

WADI ALOO

Black Bean Drops and Potato

Serves   4
Preparation time   10 minutes
Cooking time   35 minutes

These *wadis* are useful to have in your pantry; especially when you have run out of fresh vegetables and that unexpected guest rings the front doorbell! You may use additional vegetables in this preparation.

Imperial (Metric)	American
3 tablespoons ghee	3 tablespoons ghee
4 *wadis*, broken into pieces	4 *wadis*, broken into pieces
8 oz (225g) potatoes, sliced	1½ cups potatoes, sliced
Pinch of turmeric	Pinch of turmeric
½ pint (300ml) ready gravy (page 28)	1¼ cups ready gravy (page 28)
Sea salt, to taste	Sea salt, to taste
½ teaspoon garam masala	½ teaspoon garam masala
1 tablespoon chopped coriander leaves	1 tablespoon chopped cilantro

1

Heat the ghee in a frying pan and sauté the *wadis* over medium heat until deep golden all over.

2

Add potatoes and turmeric, and stir thoroughly. Cook, stirring, over medium heat for 5 minutes.

3

Reheat gravy in a saucepan. Drop in *wadis* and potato; stir in sea salt to taste, cover pan, lower heat, and simmer 20 minutes.

4

Sprinkle garam masala over mixture and remove from heat.

5

Serve hot, garnished with coriander leaves.

SHALJAM ALOO AUR PAALAK

Turnip, Potato and Spinach

Serves	4
Preparation time	15 minutes
Cooking time	30 minutes

This is a typical curry, served with a bread or rice dish; other vegetables can be substituted.

Imperial (Metric)	American
4 oz (100g) ghee	½ cup ghee
4 small potatoes, scraped and sliced	4 small potatoes, scraped and sliced
4 small turnips, scraped and sliced	4 small turnips, scraped and sliced
8 oz (225g) spinach, chopped	4 cups spinach, chopped
Pinch of asafoetida powder	Pinch of asafoetida powder
1 teaspoonful white cumin seeds	1 teaspoon white cumin seeds
Large pinch of turmeric	Large pinch of turmeric
2 teaspoonsful garam masala	2 teaspoons garam masala
¼ pint (150ml) natural yogurt	⅔ cup plain yogurt
½ pint (300ml) water	1¼ cups water
Sea salt and cayenne pepper, to taste	Sea salt and cayenne pepper, to taste
Chopped coriander, to garnish	Chopped cilantro (coriander), to garnish

1

Heat half the ghee and sauté vegetables over medium heat for about 5 minutes. Then remove from pan and reserve.

2

Place the remaining ghee in a saucepan and sauté asafoetida and cumin until cumin changes colour. Stir in turmeric and garam masala and blend thoroughly.

3

Add reserved vegetables, yogurt and water and stir in. Add salt and cayenne pepper, cover pan and simmer about 20 minutes, until vegetables are done.

4

Serve hot, garnished with coriander leaves.

BAIGAN AUR TAMAATAR

Curried Aubergines (Eggplant) and Tomato

Serves	*4*
Preparation time	*15 minutes*
Cooking time	*25 minutes*

This is a typical Northern Indian dish — not too hot, not too bland. Use fresh aubergines (eggplant) in this recipe and serve with a rice dish. Do not overcook, or the aubergines (eggplant) will disintegrate!

Imperial (Metric)	American
1 lb (450g) aubergines	1 pound eggplant
4 tablespoonsful ghee	4 tablespoons ghee
1 small onion, finely chopped	1 small onion, finely chopped
2 small cloves garlic, sliced	2 small cloves garlic, sliced
½ teaspoonful turmeric	½ teaspoon turmeric
2 bay leaves	2 bay leaves
1 (1-inch/2.5cm) cinnamon stick	1 (1-inch) cinnamon stick
2 teaspoonsful sea salt (or to taste)	2 teaspoons sea salt (or to taste)
1 teaspoonful cayenne pepper	1 teaspoon cayenne pepper
Pinch of grated, fresh ginger root	Pinch of grated, fresh ginger root
5 tablespoonsful natural yogurt	⅓ cup plain yogurt
4 medium-sized tomatoes, quartered	4 medium-sized tomatoes
1 teaspoonful garam masala	1 teaspoon garam masala

1

Wash and slice the aubergines (eggplant).

2

Heat the ghee in a saucepan and sauté the onion and garlic until transparent. Add the turmeric, bay leaves and cinnamon and stir thoroughly for 2 minutes.

3

Stir in aubergine (eggplant); add salt, cayenne pepper and ginger, and blend well. Pour in the yogurt and bring to a boil — cook 10 minutes or so.

4

Add tomatoes, cover pan and continue cooking another 10 minutes, or until the aubergine (eggplant) is done.

5

Sprinkle the preparation with garam masala before serving.

CHANE KI TARKAARI

Curried Chick Peas

Serves 4

Preparation time 15 minutes plus overnight soaking

Cooking time 40 minutes

This is a robust curry dish; you may serve it with a rice or bread dish. Particularly suitable for those with a strong digestive system!

Imperial (Metric)	American
8 oz (225g) chick peas	1 cup chick peas
3 tablespoonsful ghee	3 tablespoons ghee
1 medium-sized onion, sliced	1 medium-sized onion, sliced
2 cloves garlic, sliced	2 cloves garlic, sliced
2 bay leaves	2 bay leaves
2 cloves	2 cloves
½ teaspoonful grated fresh root ginger	½ teaspoon grated, fresh ginger root
1 green chilli, chopped	1 green chili pepper, chopped
¼ pint (150ml) natural yogurt	⅔ cup plain yogurt
½ pint (300ml) water	1¼ cups water
Sea salt and pepper, to taste	Sea salt and pepper, to taste
2 tomatoes, quartered	2 tomatoes, quartered
1 teaspoonful garam masala	1 teaspoon garam masala

1

Wash and soak the chick peas. Leave half of them whole and grind the rest.

2

Heat the ghee and sauté the onion and garlic until transparent. Add bay leaves, cloves, ginger and chilli, and stir well.

3

Stir in both the whole and ground chick peas and blend a couple of minutes. Add yogurt, and cook for 2 minutes over medium heat.

4

Pour in water and add seasoning; bring to a boil. Add tomatoes, cover pan, lower heat, and simmer 20 minutes or so until chick peas are tender.

5

Serve hot, sprinkled with garam masala.

MUNGORI TAMAATAR

Mung Bean Drops and Tomato

Serves	*4*
Preparation time	*10 minutes*
Cooking time	*25 minutes*

Like *wadis*, these are made and stored in advance, and serve the same purpose! The curried *mungoris* are light on the stomach and have a splendidly exotic taste.

Imperial (Metric)	American
4 tablespoonsful ghee	4 tablespoons ghee
1 tablespoonful chopped onion	1 tablespoon chopped onion
Pinch of turmeric	Pinch of turmeric
½ teaspoonful garam masala	½ teaspoon garam masala
2 bay leaves	2 bay leaves
Pinch of grated, fresh ginger root	Pinch of grated, fresh ginger root
8 oz (225g) mung bean drops	1 cup mung bean drops
½ pint (300ml) ready gravy (page 28)	1¼ cups ready gravy (page 28)
4 fresh tomatoes, quartered	4 fresh tomatoes, quartered
Sea salt, to taste	Sea salt, to taste
½ teaspoonful green mango powder	½ teaspoon green mango powder
Chopped coriander leaves, to garnish	Chopped cilantro, to garnish

1

Heat the ghee in a frying pan and sauté the onion until transparent. Add turmeric, garam masala, bay leaves and ginger, and stir well for 2 minutes.

2

Add mung bean drops and blend well; cook, stirring, over medium heat for 5 to 7 minutes.

3

Reheat gravy in a saucepan over medium heat. Add spiced bean drops and tomatoes and add sea salt to taste. Cover pan, lower heat and cook for about 15 minutes.

4

Sprinkle with mango powder and remove from heat.

5

Serve hot, topped with coriander leaves.

BESAN KADHI

Chick Pea Fritter Curry

Serves   4

Preparation time   15 minutes plus 20 minutes resting time

Cooking time   30 minutes

Kadhi is made in many different ways; this is just one version. Serve with boiled brown rice.

Imperial (Metric)	American
4 oz (100g) chick pea flour	1 cup chick pea flour
Water, as necessary	Water, as necessary
Mustard oil, as necessary	Mustard oil, as necessary
½ pint (300ml) natural yogurt	1¼ cups plain yogurt
2 teaspoonsful mustard seeds	2 teaspoons mustard seeds
1 teaspoonful turmeric	1 teaspoon turmeric
Sea salt, to taste	Sea salt, to taste
1 green chilli, finely chopped	1 green chili pepper, finely chopped
1 tablespoonful ghee	1 tablespoon ghee
1 teaspoonful cayenne pepper	1 teaspoon cayenne pepper

1

Place the chick pea flour in a deep bowl. Add water as necessary and beat into a thick batter. Then let rest for about 20 minutes.

2

Heat sufficient oil in a *kadhai* or a deep frying pan nearly to smoking point. Drop 1 teaspoon batter into *kadhai*, then another, leaving space between them — drop several in one go. Stir them about with a *jhanna* and these drops will swell up into amorphous shapes. When they are golden all over, remove and place on a plate. They are known as *phuloris* — of the *pakoda* clan. Make 16 *phuloris*. (There will be batter left over.)

3

Place yogurt in a bowl; add leftover batter and water as necessary to make a thin mixture.

4

Heat 1 tablespoon oil in a *kadhai*, or a separate saucepan, to a high temperature. Stir in mustard seeds and cover pan to stop seeds popping out. Then stir in turmeric, salt and green chili. Pour in yogurt mixture and simmer 10 minutes.

5

Add *phuloris*, cover pan, lower heat and cook another 10 minutes, and your *kadhi* will be ready.

6

Heat ghee separately and add cayenne pepper. Sprinkle over each serving.

KEEMA MATAR AUR MAKHAANE

Minced Peas and Lotus Puffs

Serves	4
Preparation time	20 minutes
Cooking time	30 minutes

This dish is exquisite in taste and finds favour with diners of all persuasions! Of course, there is room for experimentation. This dish is moist when ready; feel free to adjust the liquid. Serve with a rice or bread dish.

Imperial (Metric)	American
2 oz (50g) lotus puffs (*makhaanas*)*	2 oz lotus puffs (*makhaanas*)*
12 oz (350g) green peas	2 cups green peas
4 oz (100g) ghee	¼ cup ghee
1 small onion, finely chopped	1 small onion, finely chopped
1 clove garlic, sliced	1 clove garlic, sliced
1 green chilli, chopped	1 green chili pepper, chopped
1 teaspoonful garam masala	1 teaspoon garam masala
½ teaspoonful grated fresh root ginger	½ teaspoon grated, fresh ginger root
½ pint (300ml) water	1¼ cups water
2 teaspoonsful sea salt (or to taste)	2 teaspoons sea salt (or to taste)
1 teaspoonful green mango powder	1 teaspoon green mango powder
Pinch of green cardamom powder	Pinch of green cardamom powder

*Roasted lotus seeds.

1

First chop the *makhaanas* into small pieces, then coarsely grind the peas.

2

Heat 2 tablespoons ghee in a *kadhai* and sauté lotus puffs until golden. Remove and place on a plate.

3

In the same *kadhai*, or saucepan, add another 2 tablespoons ghee and sauté peas gently for 5 minutes, until grains of peas start to separate. Remove and set aside.

4

Place remaining ghee in a saucepan and sauté onion and garlic until transparent. Then add chilli, garam masala and fresh ginger, and stir-fry a good 2 minutes.

5

Add lotus puffs and peas to sautéing herbs and spices, and stir-fry 5 minutes. Pour in water, stir in salt, and simmer 10 minutes, stirring occasionally.

6

Sprinkle with mango and cardamom powders, and serve hot.

JHALFARAAZI

Indian Ratatouille

Serves 4
Preparation time   10 minutes plus 30 minutes resting time
Cooking time   25 minutes

This intriguing curry dish should please one and all! By tradition, this dish includes meat, but I think you will like my recipe for a vegetarian version. Serve with a *puri* or *parauntha*.

Imperial (Metric)	American
1 large aubergine	1 large eggplant
1 courgette	1 zucchini
2 medium-sized potatoes	2 medium-sized potatoes
4 cauliflower florets	4 cauliflower florets
2 green peppers	2 green peppers
Sea salt, as required	Sea salt, as required
3 tablespoonsful ghee	3 tablespoons ghee
3 tablespoonsful chopped onion	3 tablespoons chopped onion
2 cloves of garlic, sliced	2 cloves of garlic, sliced
½ teaspoonful grated fresh root ginger	½ teaspoon grated, fresh ginger root
2 green chillies, finely chopped	2 green chili peppers, finely chopped
2 tomatoes, sliced	2 tomatoes, sliced
¼ pint (150ml) natural yogurt	⅔ cup plain yogurt
½ teaspoonful garam masala	½ teaspoon garam masala
1 tablespoonful chopped coriander leaves	1 tablespoon chopped cilantro (coriander)

1

Slice the aubergine (eggplant), courgette (zucchini), potatoes, cauliflower and green peppers; sprinkle with 2 teaspoons sea salt and let rest 30 minutes; then rinse and pat dry.

2

Heat the ghee in a saucepan and sauté the onion and garlic until transparent. Then add ginger, chillies and tomatoes — one by one — and blend well; cook for about 5 minutes.

3

Stir in sliced vegetables and mix well. Cook about 5 minutes. Add yogurt and sea salt to taste. Cover pan and simmer 10 to 15 minutes until vegetables are tender.

4

Sprinkle with garam masala and garnish with coriander leaves; serve hot.

TORAI AUR SIMLA MIRCH

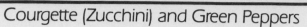

Courgette (Zucchini) and Green Peppers

Serves	4
Preparation time	10 minutes
Cooking time	30 minutes

This is a *do-piazza* dish, which means it has a preponderance of onions. The dish is moist when ready, but you may adjust the liquid. Serve it with *puri* or *parauntha*.

Imperial (Metric)	American
3 tablespoonsful ghee	3 tablespoons ghee
4 medium-sized onions, sliced	4 medium-sized onions, sliced
1 clove garlic, sliced	1 clove garlic, sliced
½ teaspoonful turmeric	½ teaspoon turmeric
1 teaspoonful garam masala	1 teaspoon garam masala
8 oz (225g) courgettes, sliced	1¾ cups zucchini, sliced
8 oz (225g) green peppers, sliced	1 cup green peppers, sliced
¼ pint (150ml) natural yogurt	⅔ cup plain yogurt
2 teaspoonsful sea salt (or to taste)	2 teaspoons sea salt (or to taste)
1 teaspoonful cayenne pepper	1 teaspoon cayenne pepper
¼ pint (150ml) water	⅔ cup water
Chopped coriander leaves, to serve	Chopped cilantro (coriander), to serve

1

Heat the ghee in a saucepan over medium heat, and sauté half the onion and garlic until they are transparent. Stir in turmeric and garam masala and blend thoroughly 2 minutes.

2

Add courgettes (zucchini), peppers and remaining onion, and stir-fry for 5 minutes.

3

Mix in yogurt, stir in the salt and cayenne pepper, and cook another 5 minutes.

4

Pour in water and simmer (without boiling) about 15 minutes, until liquid attains desired consistency.

5

Serve hot, sprinkled with coriander leaves.

PAALAK KE KOFTE

Spinach Ball Curry

Serves	4
Preparation time	15 minutes
Cooking time	25 minutes

This creamy curry will please the most finicky connoisseurs. Serve with any rice or bread preparation.

Imperial (Metric)	American
8 oz (225g) spinach	4 cups spinach
2 medium-sized potatoes	2 medium-sized potatoes
4 oz (100g) chick pea flour	1 cup chick pea flour
3 tablespoonsful double cream	3 tablespoons heavy cream
1 teaspoonful sea salt (or to taste)	1 teaspoon sea salt (or to taste)
Pinch of turmeric	Pinch of turmeric
½ teaspoonful garam masala	½ teaspoon garam masala
½ teaspoonful green mango powder	½ teaspoon green mango powder
½ teaspoonful cayenne pepper	½ teaspoon cayenne pepper
Ghee, for deep-frying	Ghee, for deep-frying
Desiccated coconut, to coat	Dried coconut, to coat
½ pint (300ml) ready gravy (page 28)	1¼ cups ready gravy (page 28)
Chopped coriander leaves, to garnish	Chopped cilantro (coriander), to garnish

1

Boil the spinach and potatoes; drain off water, peel potatoes, and grind with spinach.

2

Add chick pea flour to spinach-potato mixture and blend. Then stir in cream, salt, turmeric, garam masala, mango powder and cayenne pepper, and mix together to make a smooth dough. Pluck off small pieces and shape as desired.

3

Heat sufficient ghee in a *kadhai* or a deep fryer, roll each ball in coconut, and deep-fry until golden all over. Remove and place on a large plate.

4

Reheat gravy in a saucepan over medium heat. Carefully drop in *koftas*, cover pan, lower heat, and cook about 10 minutes.

5

Garnish with coriander leaves and serve hot.

KAMAL KAKDI KE KOFTE

Lotus Stem Balls

Serves	4
Preparation time	15 minutes
Cooking time	25 minutes

A delightful preparation, with a scrumptious taste. Serve with a rice or bread dish. It helps greatly if you make the gravy separately and in advance (see page 28).

Imperial (Metric)	American
8 oz (225g) lotus stems	½ pound lotus stems
2 oz (50g) chick pea flour	½ cup chick pea flour
1 teaspoonful sea salt (or to taste)	1 teaspoon sea salt (or to taste)
1 tablespoonful grated onion	1 tablespoon grated onion
Pinch of grated, fresh ginger root	Pinch of grated, fresh ginger root
1 green chilli, finely chopped	1 green chili pepper, finely chopped
1 teaspoonful green mango powder	1 teaspoon green mango powder
Ghee, for deep-frying	Ghee, for deep-frying
½ pint (300ml) ready gravy (page 28)	1¼ cups ready gravy (page 28)
1 tablespoonful chopped coriander leaves	1 tablespoon chopped cilantro (coriander)

1

Boil the lotus stems; drain off the water and mash the stems into a smooth mixture.

2

Place mashed lotus stems in a bowl; mix in chick pea flour, salt, onion, ginger, chilli and mango powder. Blend thoroughly into a dough and form into small balls.

3

Heat sufficient ghee in a *kadhai*, or a deep fryer, over moderate heat. Deep-fry balls — a few at a time — until golden all over. When cooked, remove and drain on paper towels.

4

Reheat the ready gravy in a saucepan over medium heat. Carefully drop balls (*koftas*) into saucepan. Cover pan, lower heat and cook about 10 minutes.

5

Serve hot, sprinkled with coriander leaves.

KELE KE KOFTE

Banana (Plantain) Ball Curry

Serves 4
Preparation time   10 minutes
Cooking time   30 minutes

This is an excellent offering from the Indian *kofta* artistes; it will be a valuable addition to your culinary repertoire. Why not delight that discerning guest?

Imperial (Metric)	American
4 green bananas (plantains)	4 plantains
2 oz (50g) wholemeal flour	½ cup whole wheat flour
½ teaspoonful sea salt (or to taste)	½ teaspoon sea salt (or to taste)
1 green chilli, chopped	1 green chili pepper, chopped
1 small onion, finely chopped	1 small onion, finely chopped
1 clove garlic, chopped	1 clove garlic, chopped
Ghee, for deep-frying	Ghee, for deep-frying
Wholemeal breadcrumbs, to coat	Whole wheat breadcrumbs, to coat
½ pint (300ml) ready gravy (page 28)	1 cup ready gravy (page 28)
1 teaspoonful garam masala	1 teaspoon garam masala

1

Boil the bananas (plantains), then peel and mash them.

2

Place the mashed bananas in a bowl; add flour, salt, chilli, onion and garlic, and knead into a smooth mixture. Pluck off small pieces and make desired shapes.

3

Heat sufficient ghee in a *kadhai* or a deep fryer over moderate heat. Roll each shape (*kofta*) in the breadcrumbs, and deep-fry until golden all over; cook a few at a time. When cooked, place on a plate and put to one side.

4

Reheat gravy in a saucepan over moderate heat. Carefully drop in *koftas*, cover pan and simmer about 10 minutes.

5

Sprinkle mixture with garam masala just before serving.

Chapter 7

Sukhi Sabziyaan
Side Dishes

Indian cuisine includes a tremendous repertoire of side dishes. These dishes please the palate and, by their almost infinite variety, pungency and exoticism, offer a taste for every tongue! The dry dishes uplift an Indian meal and, because several of these dishes are included in one meal, they emphasize the rich sumptuousness of Indian meals and add colour to the proceedings into the bargain!

The master chefs of India have evolved a large variety of these stylish dishes. Side dishes can be grouped into several distinct compartments: there are the "whole" dishes, which combine delicious taste with distinctive looks; there are the "stuffed" dishes, which lend themselves to experimentation and reach a pinnacle of culinary perfection; *bhurtas* are another category of dishes, which are made by roasting and boiling the vegetables and fruits and then mashing and spicing them. And, of course, the basic *bhaajis* are fried vegetables, made in large numbers even for one meal in some Indian homes. All in all, these side dishes provide a wide range of flavours and colours for your dining table.

I have included a few recipes from each of the categories in the expectation that they will delight both the readers and their friends and families.

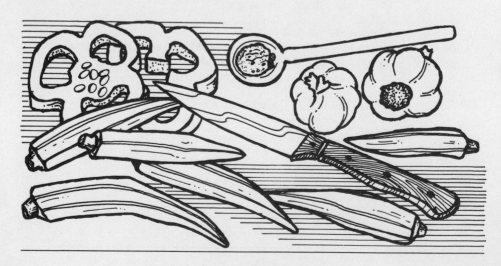

BHINDI BHAAJI

Fried "Ladies' Fingers" (Okra)

Serves 6
Preparation time 10 minutes
Cooking time 30 minutes

Bhindis or "Ladies' Fingers" are popularly known as okra, too. This delicious dry preparation is served as a side dish with a meal, or on its own with one of the fried breads.

Imperial (Metric)	American
1 lb (450g) okra	1 pound okra
5 tablespoonsful mustard oil	⅓ cup mustard oil
2 medium-sized onions, finely sliced	2 medium-sized onions, finely sliced
2 cloves garlic, sliced	2 cloves garlic, sliced
½ teaspoonful turmeric	½ teaspoon turmeric
Sea salt, to taste	Sea salt, to taste
1 teaspoonful cayenne pepper	1 teaspoon cayenne pepper
1 teaspoonful green mango powder	1 teaspoon green mango powder
1 deseeded green pepper, cut into rings	1 seeded green pepper, cut into rings

1

Wash the okra and chop off tops. Then cut into thin rounds.

2

Heat the oil in a *kadhai* or saucepan and sauté half the onion and garlic in the mustard oil until golden. Add turmeric and stir-fry over moderate heat about 2 minutes.

3

Add okra together with remaining onion, stir in salt and cayenne pepper and stir until well blended. Cover pan, lower heat and cook thoroughly, for about 20 minutes, stirring from time to time.

4

Before removing pan from heat, sprinkle with mango powder, scatter pepper rings over mixture, and cook, covered, another 5 minutes. Serve hot.

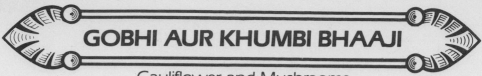

GOBHI AUR KHUMBI BHAAJI

Cauliflower and Mushrooms

Serves 4
Preparation time   10 minutes
Cooking time   35 minutes

This is a very popular seasonal vegetable preparation in India. It can be made into *bhaaji* or curry; this dry preparation is a marvellous side dish.

Imperial (Metric)	American
Water, as necessary	Water, as necessary
8 oz (225g) cauliflower florets	2¼ cups cauliflower florets
8 oz (225g) mushrooms, halved	2¼ cups mushrooms, halved
5 tablespoonsful ghee	5 tablespoons ghee
Pinch of asafoetida powder	Pinch of asafoetida powder
3 tablespoonsful chopped onion	3 tablespoons chopped onion
1 teaspoonful sliced fresh root ginger	1 teaspoon sliced, fresh ginger root
3 tablespoonsful coriander leaves	3 tablespoons cilantro (coriander)
1 green chilli, crushed	1 green chili pepper, crushed
1 teaspoonful garam masala	1 teaspoon garam masala
4 tomatoes, quartered	4 tomatoes, quartered
Sea salt, to taste	Sea salt, to taste
1 teaspoonful green mango powder	1 teaspoon green mango powder

1

Boil enough water to cook the cauliflower and mushrooms, add both vegetables, and cook 5 minutes. Drain and set aside.

2

Heat half the ghee in a *kadhai* or saucepan and sauté cauliflower and mushrooms lightly for 5 minutes over moderate heat. Remove and set aside.

3

Add remaining ghee to saucepan and sauté asafoetida and onion until golden. Remove onion with a slotted spoon.

4

Make a paste by grinding together ginger, coriander leaves, chilli and garam masala. In the ghee still remaining in the pan, sauté the paste, over medium heat, for about 3 minutes.

5

Return onion, cauliflower and mushrooms to saucepan. Stir well. Add tomatoes and stir into sauce. Cover pan, lower heat and cook 10 to 15 minutes.

6

Sprinkle with mango powder and remove pan from heat.

7

Serve hot.

MATAR AUR KARAMKALLA

Peas and Cabbage

Serves	*4*
Preparation time	*10 minutes*
Cooking time	*15 minutes*

This tasty *bhaaji* preparation may be served with one of the fried bread dishes, or as a side dish with a main meal.

Imperial (Metric)	American
3 tablespoonsful ghee	3 tablespoons ghee
1 medium-sized onion, sliced	1 medium-sized onion, sliced
½ teaspoonful grated fresh root ginger	½ teaspoon grated, fresh ginger root
1 green chilli, chopped	1 green chili pepper, chopped
½ teaspoonful turmeric	½ teaspoon turmeric
6 oz (175g) green peas	1 cup shelled peas
8 oz (225g) shredded cabbage	3 cups shredded cabbage
Sea salt, to taste	Sea salt, to taste
Water, as necessary	Water, as necessary
½ teaspoonful garam masala	½ teaspoon garam masala

1

Heat the ghee in a *kadhai* or saucepan and sauté the onion, ginger and chilli until onion is golden. Add turmeric and stir-fry a minute or so.

2

Add peas, cabbage, salt and a few spoons of water, cover pan, lower heat and cook 10 minutes, until cabbage is cooked but still crisp.

3

Sprinkle with garam masala, stir once or twice, and remove pan from heat.

4

Serve hot.

ARBI BHAAJI

Fried Yams

Serves	6
Preparation time	10 *minutes*
Cooking time	20 *minutes*

Arbis are also known as yams. This preparation is a delightful side dish, also served on its own with a *kachauri* — stuffed *puri*.

Imperial (Metric)	American
1 lb (450g) yams	1 pound yams
3 tablespoonsful ghee	3 tablespoons ghee
Pinch of asafoetida powder	Pinch of asafoetida powder
2 teaspoonsful carom seeds (*ajwain*)	2 teaspoons carom seeds (*ajwain*)
Pinch of turmeric	Pinch of turmeric
Sea salt, to taste	Sea salt, to taste
Large pinch of cayenne pepper	Large pinch of cayenne pepper
Water as necessary	Water as necessary
1 tablespoonful lemon juice	1 tablespoon lemon juice

1

Scrape the yams and thinly slice them. Carefully wash slices; then drain and set aside.

2

Heat the ghee in a *kadhai* and sauté the asafoetida and carom seeds until golden. Stir in turmeric and cook over medium heat about 2 minutes.

3

Add yams, stir in the salt and cayenne, and blend thoroughly. Add a few spoons of water, cover the pan, and cook about 15 minutes, until yams are soft. Stir occasionally.

4

Sprinkle with lemon juice and stir a few times before removing *kadhai* from heat.

5

Serve hot or cold.

PANEER AUR MOOLI KA SAAG

Cream Cheese and Radish Leaves

Serves	4
Preparation time	15 minutes
Cooking time	20 minutes

Try to obtain the leaves from white radish (*mooli*), and you will have a real delicacy on your table! Alternatively, use ordinary red radish leaves. Serve as a side dish with a main meal.

Imperial (Metric)	American
8 oz (225g) radish leaves, chopped	4 cups radish leaves, chopped
3 tablespoonsful ghee	3 tablespoons ghee
8 oz (225g) home-made cream cheese, cubed	1 cup homemade cream cheese, cubed
1 tablespoonful chopped onion	1 tablespoon chopped onion
2 cloves garlic, sliced	2 cloves garlic, sliced
½ teaspoonful ground coriander	½ teaspoon ground coriander
Sea salt, to taste	Sea salt, to taste
1 teaspoonful cayenne pepper	1 teaspoon cayenne pepper
Water, as necessary	Water, as necessary
1 teaspoonful green mango powder	1 teaspoon green mango powder

1

Boil the radish leaves. Drain and set aside.

2

Heat 1 tablespoon ghee in a *kadhai* or saucepan and sauté the cheese cubes until golden. Remove and set aside.

3

Add remaining ghee to the pan and sauté onion and garlic until golden. Add the coriander, salt and cayenne pepper and stir-fry over moderate heat for 2 to 3 minutes.

4

Add sautéed cheese and radish leaves to the mixture and carefully stir a few times. Add a few spoons of water, cover pan, lower heat, and cook about 10 minutes.

5

Sprinkle mango powder over preparation before removing pan from heat. Serve hot.

POORE KELE

Whole Green Bananas (Plantains)

Serves	4
Preparation time	15 minutes
Cooking time	40 minutes

This is a delightful if unusual dish. Once you get used to its mild taste, you will be hooked on it. Serve with a *puri* or *parauntha* dish.

Imperial (Metric)	American
4 green bananas (plantains), unpeeled	4 green bananas (plantains), unpeeled
Water, as necessary	Water, as necessary
4 tablespoonsful ghee	4 tablespoons ghee
1 tablespoonful chopped onion	1 tablespoon chopped onion
2 bay leaves	2 bay leaves
½ teaspoonful turmeric	½ teaspoon turmeric
2 cloves	2 cloves
4 black peppercorns	4 black peppercorns
5 tablespoonsful natural yogurt	⅓ cup plain yogurt
Sea salt, to taste	Sea salt, to taste
1 teaspoonful cayenne pepper	1 teaspoon cayenne pepper
1 teaspoonful garam masala	1 teaspoon garam masala

1

Cut off the stems and boil whole, unpeeled bananas (plantains) in water. Drain.

2

Prick bananas (plantains) all over with a fork or cocktail stick (toothpick).

3

Heat the ghee in a saucepan and sauté bananas (plantains) until golden. Remove and set aside.

4

In the ghee still in the pan, sauté onion until golden. Add bay leaves, turmeric, cloves and peppercorns, and stir thoroughly.

5

Return bananas (plantains) to the pan, carefully stir in yogurt, and add 4 tablespoons water. Stir in salt and cayenne pepper, cover pan, and simmer over moderate heat for about 20 minutes, until bananas (plantains) are tender. Stir mixture from time to time, taking care not to break bananas (plantains). Serve hot, sprinkled with the garam masala.

SAABUT GOBHI

Whole Cauliflower

Serves	4
Preparation time	10 minutes
Cooking time	40 minutes

The "whole" or "musallam" dishes are a delicious Mughal speciality. They are usually served with a main meal, in addition to one or more curried dishes.

Imperial (Metric)	American
2 tablespoonsful ghee	2 tablespoons ghee
2 tomatoes, quartered	2 tomatoes, quartered
2 bay leaves	2 bay leaves
1½ teaspoonsful garam masala	1½ teaspoons garam masala
1½ teaspoonsful turmeric	1½ teaspoons turmeric
½ teaspoonful cayenne pepper	½ teaspoon cayenne pepper
Sea salt, to taste	Sea salt, to taste
1 tablespoonful desiccated coconut	1 tablespoon dried coconut
One 2 lb (900g) cauliflower	One 2 pound cauliflower
¼ pint (150ml) water	⅔ cup water
Chopped coriander leaves and lemon slices, to garnish	Chopped cilantro (coriander) and lemon slices, to garnish

1

Heat the ghee in a deep saucepan and sauté tomatoes until their juices run. Add bay leaves, garam masala, turmeric, cayenne pepper, salt and coconut and stir thoroughly another 2 to 3 minutes.

2

Remove leaves and stem from cauliflower, turn it floret-side down, and place over cooking mixture.

3

Pour in water, cover pan, and simmer about 30 minutes. From time to time, remove cover and baste cauliflower with cooking mixture.

4

When cauliflower is tender, remove from heat and transfer the whole cauliflower together with the remaining liquid onto a serving dish.

5

Garnish with coriander and lemon and serve hot.

SAMUCHI LAUKI

Whole Marrow (Squash)

Serves	6
Preparation time	10 minutes
Cooking time	35 minutes

An exciting preparation to pamper your palate and known for its mildness! It is a relatively dry dish and should be served as part of the main meal, in the company of other curried fare.

Imperial (Metric)	American
1 medium-sized long marrow	1 medium-sized squash
1½ pints (900ml) tepid water	3¾ cups tepid water
8 tablespoonsful ghee	½ cup ghee
1 medium-sized onion, finely chopped	1 medium-sized onion, finely chopped
4 small bay leaves	4 small bay leaves
1 small onion, grated	1 small onion, grated
2 cloves garlic, crushed	2 cloves garlic, crushed
1 (1-inch/2.5cm) piece fresh root ginger	1 (1-inch) piece fresh ginger root
1 teaspoonful turmeric	1 teaspoon turmeric
½ teaspoonful cayenne pepper	½ teaspoon cayenne pepper
1 teaspoonful white cumin seeds	1 teaspoon white cumin seeds
8 tablespoonsful natural yogurt	½ cup plain yogurt
2 tomatoes, chopped	2 tomatoes, chopped
2 teaspoonsful sea salt (or to taste)	2 teaspoons sea salt (or to taste)
1 teaspoonful garam masala	1 teaspoon garam masala
1 tablespoonful chopped fresh mint	1 tablespoon chopped, fresh mint

1

Peel the marrow (squash) and make several gashes in it with a knife.

2

Then place it (without breaking or cutting) in a large saucepan with the tepid water. Cover and cook over moderate heat about 5 minutes. Drain.

3

Heat ghee in a suitable saucepan and sauté chopped onion and bay leaves over moderate heat until golden.

4

Meanwhile, make a paste with grated onion, garlic, ginger, turmeric and cayenne pepper by grinding them together.

5

Reduce heat. Stir in cumin seeds and the paste, and sauté about 10 minutes until ghee separates. Add yogurt, tomato and sea salt, and stir a few times.

6

Slide marrow (squash) into pan and carefully turn over so that it is covered on all sides with the mixture. Cover tightly and cook over low heat about 15 minutes.

7

Serve hot, sprinkled with garam masala and chopped mint.

111

SAABUT ALOO

Whole Potatoes

Serves 4
Preparation time   15 minutes plus 30 minutes soaking time
Cooking time   30 minutes

This preparation is a particular favourite of my family. Serve it with one of the fried breads, or as part of the main meal.

Imperial (Metric)	American
8 oz (225g) small potatoes	6 to 8 small potatoes
Water, as necessary	Water, as necessary
4 oz (100g) ghee	½ cup ghee
Pinch of turmeric	Pinch of turmeric
2 bay leaves	2 bay leaves
1 small onion, grated	1 small onion, grated
1 (½-inch/1.25cm) piece fresh root ginger, crushed	1 (½-inch) piece fresh ginger root, crushed
2 green chillies, chopped	2 green chili peppers, chopped
8 tablespoonsful natural yogurt	½ cup plain yogurt
Sea salt, to taste	Sea salt, to taste
1 teaspoonful garam masala	1 teaspoon garam masala

1

Scrape the potatoes; prick all over with a fork and wash. Then soak in salted water for about 30 minutes.

2

Heat half the ghee in a saucepan and sauté potatoes until golden. Drain and set aside.

3

Add remaining ghee to pan and stir-fry turmeric and bay leaves until golden.

4

Make a paste by grinding together onion, ginger, chillies and garlic. Mix into turmeric and keep stirring until mixture stops sticking to the pan's surface.

5

Stir in yogurt and salt, and cook over moderate heat for 2 minutes.

6

Add potatoes, cover pan and cook another 10 to 15 minutes until potatoes are done. Stir from time to time, and lower heat after first 5 minutes. Add a few spoons of water if the mixture becomes too dry for your liking.

7

Sprinkle garam masala over mixture 2 minutes before removing pan from heat, and blend well.

8

Serve hot or cold.

ALOO TAMAATAR BHURTA

Mashed Potato and Tomato

Serves	6
Preparation time	10 minutes
Cooking time	25 minutes

This quickly prepared side dish is not just a pretty face; it is appetizing, too. And it is nothing like the mashed potato of the West!

Imperial (Metric)	American
1 lb (450g) potatoes	1 pound potatoes
4 tablespoonsful ghee	4 tablespoons ghee
4 spring onions, chopped	4 scallions, chopped
2 cloves garlic, sliced	2 cloves garlic, sliced
4 tomatoes, quartered	4 tomatoes, quartered
1 teaspoonful garam masala	1 teaspoon garam masala
1 teaspoonful chilli powder	1 teaspoon chili powder
1 teaspoonful grated fresh root ginger	1 teaspoon grated, fresh ginger root
Sea salt, to taste	Sea salt, to taste
1 tablespoonful chopped coriander leaves	1 tablespoon chopped cilantro (coriander)

1

Boil, peel and mash the potatoes.

2

Heat 2 tablespoons ghee in a *kadhai* or frying pan and sauté the onion and garlic until golden.

3

Add potato, tomatoes, garam masala, chilli powder, ginger and sea salt, and blend together over low heat for about 10 minutes.

4

Remove from heat, sprinkle with remaining ghee, and garnish with coriander.

5

Serve hot or cold.

BHAANTE KA BHURTA

Aubergine (Eggplant) Smasher

Serves	6
Preparation time	10 minutes
Cooking time	25 minutes

Essentially a side dish, made from round aubergines (eggplant). Its taste is pungent and refreshingly exotic.

Imperial (Metric)	American
One 1 lb (450g) round aubergine	One 1 pound round eggplant
4 cloves garlic, peeled	4 cloves garlic, peeled
1 teaspoonful grated fresh root ginger	1 teaspoon grated ginger root
Sea salt, to taste	Sea salt, to taste
2 green chillies, chopped	2 green chili peppers, chopped
1 tablespoonful chopped onion	1 tablespoon chopped onion
1 tablespoonful chopped coriander leaves	1 tablespoon chopped cilantro (coriander)
½ teaspoonful garam masala	½ teaspoon garam masala

1

Wash and clean the aubergine (eggplant); cut slits in the flesh and stick in the whole garlic cloves. Dry roast until skin shrivels up.

2

When aubergine (eggplant) cools down, peel it and mash the pulp; add ginger, salt, and chillies.

3

Heat ghee and sauté onion until golden. Lower heat, add aubergines (eggplant) pulp, and stir-fry for another 10 minutes or so.

4

Sprinkle coriander and garam masala over mixture and blend.

5

Serve hot or cold.

BHARWAAN BAIGAN

Stuffed Aubergines (Eggplant)

Serves	4
Preparation time	15 minutes
Cooking time	25 minutes

This category of preparations can be baked or shallow fried and offers a lot of possibilities because you can try your hand at other vegetables! The elongated variety of aubergine (eggplant) is most suitable for this dish. Serve as a side dish with a meal.

Imperial (Metric)	American
1 tablespoonful each: anise, cumin fenugreek and coriander seeds	1 tablespoon each: anise, cumin, fenugreek and coriander seeds
1 plump tomato, quartered	1 plump tomato, quartered
3 tablespoonsful chopped onion	3 tablespoons chopped onion
1 teaspoonful green mango powder	1 teaspoon green mango powder
1½ teaspoonsful sea salt (or to taste)	1½ teaspoons sea salt (or to taste)
1 teaspoonful cayenne pepper	1 teaspoon cayenne pepper
Ghee, as necessary	Ghee, as necessary
4 long aubergines	4 long eggplants

1

Dry roast all the seeds, then grind them into a powder.

2

To the powder add tomato, onion, mango powder, salt, and cayenne pepper — one by one, in order of listing. Mix together and, adding a little ghee, make the mixture binding.

3

Clean the aubergines (eggplants) and slit them lengthways in the middle, without halving them; do not remove leafy sepals from the tops of aubergines (eggplants).

4

Stuff the vegetable-spice mixture into aubergines (eggplants); do not discard the left-over mixture.

5

Heat 1 tablespoon ghee in a large frying pan. Place aubergines (eggplant) in pan, and scatter left-over mixture around them. Lower heat, cover pan, and cook until aubergines (eggplants) are done — about 20 minutes. Keep turning aubergines (eggplants) over, and add more ghee as necessary so that the contents do not stick to the pan. Serve hot or cold.

SHALJAM BHURTA

Mashed Turnip

Serves	*6*
Preparation time	*10 minutes*
Cooking time	*25 minutes*

Bhurtas are mashed vegetables; they are made quickly and have a pungent taste with appetizing looks! Acquire a taste for these side dishes and you are hooked forever!

Imperial (Metric)	American
1 lb (450g) turnips	1 pound turnips
4 tablespoonsful ghee	4 tablespoons ghee
½ teaspoonful grated fresh root ginger	½ teaspoon grated, fresh ginger root
1 medium-sized onion, finely chopped	1 medium-sized onion, finely chopped
2 medium-sized tomatoes, quartered	2 medium-sized tomatoes, quartered
2 green chillies, chopped	2 green chili peppers, chopped
½ teaspoonful ground cumin	½ teaspoon ground cumin
1 teaspoonful garam masala	1 teaspoon garam masala
Sea salt, to taste	Sea salt, to taste
Pinch of raw cane sugar	Pinch of raw sugar
1 tablespoonful chopped coriander leaves	1 tablespoon chopped cilantro (coriander)

1

Boil, peel, and mash the turnips.

2

Heat ghee in a *kadhai* or a frying pan, and sauté the ginger and onion until golden.

3

Add tomatoes, along with chillies, cumin and garam masala. Mix in turnip, add salt, and blend.

4

Keep pan over moderate heat, and stir for about 10 minutes. Then add sugar and blend again.

5

Serve hot, topped with coriander.

PAALAK BHURTA

Mashed Spinach

Serves	6
Preparation time	10 minutes
Cooking time	25 minutes

Acquire a taste for this colourful dish, and you will know what you have been missing! Usually served as a side dish with a main meal. Adjust the quantity of ghee to your liking.

Imperial (Metric)	American
1 lb (450g) spinach	3 cups spinach
1 medium-sized parsnip	1 medium-sized parsnip
5 tablespoonsful ghee	5 tablespoons ghee
2 medium-sized onions, finely chopped	2 medium-sized onions, finely chopped
2 cloves garlic, sliced	2 cloves garlic, sliced
½ teaspoonful grated fresh root ginger	½ teaspoon grated, fresh ginger root
1 teaspoonful cayenne pepper	1 teaspoon cayenne pepper
2 tomatoes, quartered	2 tomatoes, quartered
Sea salt, to taste	Sea salt, to taste
½ teaspoonful garam masala	½ teaspoon garam masala

1

Place the spinach and parsnip in water and bring to a boil. Drain and finely chop spinach, mashing parsnip into the mixture.

2

Heat half the ghee in a *kadhai* or a saucepan, and sauté the onion and garlic until golden.

3

Add the ginger, cayenne pepper and tomatoes, and stir over moderate heat for 2 or 3 minutes. Mix in chopped spinach and parsnip, add salt, and stir-fry for 5 minutes.

4

Sprinkle with garam masala and cook, stirring, for another 3 to 5 minutes.

5

Serve hot, topped with remaining ghee.

BHARWAAN TAMAATAR

Stuffed Tomatoes

Serves	6
Preparation time	15 minutes
Cooking time	20 minutes

A very popular side dish! The filling can be varied to suit your personal taste. I hope you will like it.

Imperial (Metric)	American
6 firm, ripe tomatoes	6 firm, ripe tomatoes
8 tablespoonsful mixed vegetables, parboiled and diced	8 tablespoons mixed vegetables, parboiled and diced
2 tablespoonsful chopped coriander leaves	2 tablespoons chopped cilantro (coriander)
1 green chilli, chopped	1 green chili pepper, chopped
1 small onion, finely chopped	1 small onion, finely chopped
Pinch of grated fresh ginger root	Pinch of grated fresh ginger root
1 teaspoonful garam masala	1 teaspoon garam masala
Sea salt, to taste	Sea salt, to taste
Ghee, as necessary	Ghee, as necessary
1 teaspoonful white cumin seeds	1 teaspoon white cumin seeds

1

Slice the tops off the tomatoes and scoop out the pulp. Save tops to use as lids later.

2

In a deep bowl mix vegetables, coriander, chilli, onion, ginger, garam masala and salt — one by one; also add tomato pulp and mix thoroughly.

3

Heat 3 tablespoons ghee in a *kadhai*, or a large frying pan, and sauté cumin seeds until they change colour. Then carefully arrange tomato shells in pan, over cumin. Stuff shells with vegetable mixture. Replace tomato lids and secure with cocktail sticks (toothpicks). Sprinkle left-over mixture around tomatoes in pan. Cover pan and cook over low heat about 15 minutes. Turn tomatoes over a few times — but with great care — and add more ghee as necessary so that tomatoes do not stick to pan. Serve hot or cold.

BHARWAAN KARELE

Stuffed Bitter Gourds

| Serves 6 |
| Preparation time 20 minutes plus overnight standing time |
| Cooking time 20 minutes |

A classy side dish to be served with a main meal. Bitter gourds are becoming known in the West for their medicinal and nutritional qualities. However, the bitterness of these gourds must be removed before they are cooked.

Imperial (Metric)	American
6 bitter gourds	6 bitter gourds
Sea salt, as necessary	Sea salt, as necessary
1 teaspoonful each: fennel,	1 teaspoon each: fennel,
cumin and nigella seeds	cumin and nigella seeds
1 tablespoonful chopped onion	1 tablespoon chopped onion
½ teaspoonful chilli powder	½ teaspoon chili powder
2 teaspoonsful green mango powder	2 teaspoons green mango powder
1 teaspoonful garam masala	1 teaspoon garam masala
1 tablespoonful lemon juice	1 tablespoon lemon juice
Vegetable oil, as necessary	Vegetable oil, as necessary

1

Scrape off outer skin and slit bitter gourds lengthways without halving them. Carefully scoop out pulp from each gourd and mix it with outer scrapings.

2

Sprinkle a generous amount of salt over scooped-out flesh as well as outside and inside of gourds. Let stand overnight. Then rinse thoroughly under running water.

3

In a deep bowl, place seeds, onion, chilli powder, mango powder and garam masala. Stir in 2 teaspoons sea salt and lemon juice and blend. Also add outer skins and pulp from gourds and, adding a little oil as necessary, make a binding mixture.

4

Stuff this mixture into bitter gourds, and tie them up with thread so that the spice mixture does not escape while cooking.

5

Heat 1 tablespoon oil in a large frying pan and position the bitter gourds on it. Shallow-fry over moderate heat, adding more oil as necessary, until gourds are deep golden — about 15 minutes. Serve hot or cold. This dish tastes delicious either way!

BHARWAAN SIMLA MIRCH

Stuffed Green Peppers

Serves   4
Preparation time   10 minutes
Cooking time   30 minutes

Fillings for these dishes can always be varied to cater to personal preferences. As this dish is fairly mild, even small children can enjoy it without too much moderation.

Imperial (Metric)	*American*
4 medium-sized green peppers	4 medium-sized green peppers
Ghee, as necessary	Ghee, as necessary
1 tablespoonful finely chopped onion	1 tablespoon finely chopped onion
4 potatoes, boiled, peeled and diced	4 potatoes, boiled, peeled, and diced
½ teaspoonful grated fresh root ginger	½ teaspoon grated, fresh ginger root
4 small tomatoes, quartered	4 small tomatoes, quartered
Sea salt, to taste	Sea salt, to taste
½ teaspoonful cayenne pepper	½ teaspoon cayenne pepper
1 teaspoonful garam masala	1 teaspoon garam masala
1 tablespoonful fresh lemon juice	1 tablespoon fresh lemon juice

1

Slice the tops off the green peppers and scoop out the pulp. Reserve tops to use as lids later.

2

Heat 2 tablespoons ghee in a *kadhai,* or saucepan, and sauté onion until golden. Add remaining ingredients — one by one; also add the green pepper pulp, and blend mixture over moderate heat for 5 to 7 minutes.

3

Fill each green pepper shell with mixture. Replace tops, and secure with wooden cocktail sticks (toothpicks).

4

Heat 2 tablespoons ghee in a *kadhai,* or a large frying pan, and then carefully arrange green peppers in the pan; scatter left-over mixture around them. Cover pan, lower heat and cook until green peppers are cooked through — about 15 minutes.

5

Serve hot.

Chapter 8

Chatni, Raite, Salaad Aur Achaar
Sauces, Relishes and Pickles

The dishes in this chapter liven up a meal, however insipid and bland. All meals in India are served with one or more dishes from this section. Many of them boost the appetite and are reputed to have digestive qualities. You may serve them with western foods, too. Most of them are made quickly and are suitable for picnics and parties. Chutneys are the quickest to make, but they are nothing like their western counterparts.

Raitas are yogurt-based dishes; they are made with fruits and vegetables. Often these are served to cool down the chilli effect of curries and other accompanying hot dishes in the meal.

Salads are rather a simple and occasional pleasure with Indian meals. Although variety is of course possible, it is not a widespread practice to experiment. While salads are always made fresh, pickles can be prepared well in advance as they can last a long time. Pickles are made in many different ways and last for different periods depending on the method used. They have a contrast and pungency that perk up any meal; they also boast of stimulating the appetite and aiding digestion.

ZEERA LAHSUN KI CHATNI

Cumin and Garlic Chutney

Serves   4

Preparation time   5 minutes plus chilling time

If you like a sour chutney with your savouries, this dish is the last word!

Imperial (Metric)	American
2 teaspoonful white cumin seeds	2 teaspoons white cumin seeds
2 cloves garlic	2 cloves garlic
2 fresh green chillies	2 fresh, green chilies
Sea salt, to taste	Sea salt, to taste
5 tablespoonsful fresh lemon juice	1/3 cup fresh lemon juice

1

Coarsely grind the cumin seeds, garlic, chillies and salt.

2

Add lemon juice and stir a few times.

3

Serve chilled with whatever takes your fancy!

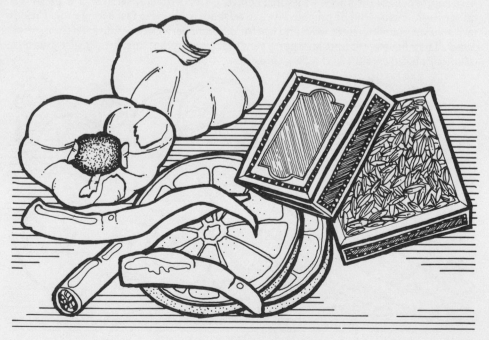

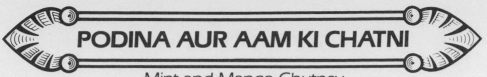

PODINA AUR AAM KI CHATNI

Mint and Mango Chutney

Serves   6

Preparation time   5 minutes plus chilling time

I am partial to this refreshing chutney and hope that you will like it, too. Left-over chutney can be stored in the refrigerator for subsequent use.

Imperial (Metric)	American
8 tablespoonsful chopped fresh mint	½ cup chopped, fresh mint
3 medium-sized green mangoes, quartered	3 medium-sized green mangoes, quartered
Pinch of asafoetida powder	Pinch of asafoetida powder
3 teaspoonsful sea salt	3 teaspoons sea salt
1 teaspoonful white cumin seeds	1 teaspoon white cumin seeds
2 fresh green chillies, halved	2 fresh green chili peppers, halved
5 tablespoonsful water	⅓ cup water

1

Place all the ingredients except the water over a *sil*, and grind coarsely with a *batta* (or use an electric grinder). Transfer chutney to a serving bowl.

2

Add water and mix thoroughly.

3

Serve chilled as a side dish.

GARI KI CHATNI

Fresh Coconut Chutney

Serves	4
Preparation time	10 minutes plus overnight soaking and chilling time
Cooking time	5 minutes

This chutney is often served with a Southern Indian dish and is usually accompanied by another sauce like *Saambhar*. Any left-over chutney can be stored in the refrigerator for later use.

Imperial (Metric)	American
1 tablespoonful each: split black beans and chick peas	1 tablespoon each: split black beans and chick peas
½ pint (300ml) natural yogurt	1¼ cups plain yogurt
Sea salt, to taste	Sea salt, to taste
½ fresh coconut, grated	½ fresh coconut, grated
2 green chillies, ground	2 green chili peppers, ground
½ teaspoonful grated fresh root ginger	½ teaspoon grated, fresh ginger root
½ tablespoonful ghee	½ tablespoon ghee
1 tablespoonful mustard seeds	1 tablespoon mustard seeds
4 curry leaves	4 curry leaves
1 tablespoonful shredded coriander leaves	1 tablespoon shredded cilantro (coriander)

1

Soak the beans and peas overnight. Drain and grind finely.

2

Beat the yogurt and salt to a smooth consistency. Add the coconut, then stir in ground beans and peas together with chillies and ginger and beat briskly.

3

Heat ghee in a *kadhai* or a saucepan. Add mustard and curry leaves and stir once or twice. Then pour in the yogurt mixture and sauté for about 2 minutes over medium heat. Remove pan from heat and transfer contents to a serving dish.

4

Stir in coriander and chill before serving.

SIRKE KI CHATNI

Vinegar Chutney

Serves 6
Preparation time   10 minutes

Many interesting vinegar concoctions are made in India; here is a quick one made with white wine vinegar.

Imperial (Metric)	*American*
½ pint (300ml) white wine vinegar	1¼ cups white wine vinegar
1 large onion, chopped	1 large onion, chopped
3 cloves garlic, grated	3 cloves garlic, grated
Sea salt, to taste	Sea salt, to taste
1 teaspoonful freshly ground	1 teaspoon freshly ground
black pepper	black pepper
1 teaspoonful raw cane sugar (optional)	1 teaspoon raw sugar (optional)

1

Place all the ingredients in a bowl and blend thoroughly.

2

For variety, add sugar; but make sure that the sugar is fully dissolved before serving.

SAAMBHAR PAANI

Sauce with Vegetables

Serves	6
Preparation time	20 minutes
Cooking time	40 minutes

This sauce is usually served with many Southern Indian dishes. Preferred seasonal vegetables can be substituted.

Imperial (Metric)	American
Section A:	*Section A:*
4 oz (100g) pigeon peas	½ cup pigeon peas
1½ pints (900ml) water	3¾ cups water
Sea salt, to taste	Sea salt, to taste
1 teaspoonful turmeric	1 teaspoon turmeric
Section B:	*Section B:*
3 tablespoonsful ghee	3 tablespoons ghee
¼ teaspoonful asafoetida powder	¼ teaspoon asafoetida powder
1 teaspoonful wholegrain mustard	1 teaspoon whole grain mustard
12 curry leaves	12 curry leaves
6 black peppercorns, whole	6 black peppercorns, whole
½ teaspoonful pounded red chillies	½ teaspoon pounded red chili peppers
Section C:	*Section C:*
Clean and cut the following into convenient pieces:	Clean and cut the following into convenient pieces:
1 turnip	1 turnip
2 medium-sized potatoes	2 medium-sized potatoes
1 medium-sized aubergine	1 medium-sized eggplant
1 medium-sized onion	1 medium-sized onion
2 green chillies	2 green chili peppers
4 oz (100g) pumpkin	¾ cup pumpkin
Section D:	*Section D:*
1 tablespoonful *saambhar* powder	1 tablespoon *saambhar* powder
2 medium-sized tomatoes, diced	2 medium-sized tomatoes, diced
1½ tablespoonsful each: chick peas and black beans, roasted and ground	1½ tablespoons each: chick peas and black beans, roasted and ground
2 tablespoonsful tamarind juice	2 tablespoons tamarind juice

Section E:
1 tablespoonful fresh lemon juice
1 tablespoonful coriander leaves,
     finely chopped
2 teaspoonsful desiccated coconut

Section E:
1 tablespoon fresh lemon juice
1 tablespoon cilantro (coriander),
     finely chopped
2 teaspoons dried coconut

1

Clean and wash the pigeon peas. Place in a saucepan, add water, salt and turmeric, and cook over medium heat about 20 minutes; leave pan half-covered.

2

While peas are cooking, heat ghee in a separate saucepan. Add all the ingredients listed in Section B, one by one, and stir several times. Then toss in vegetables listed in Section C, and sauté over low heat about 5 minutes.

3

By now the pigeon peas should be nearly cooked. Transfer the pan with the vegetables. Then add *saambhar* powder, tomatoes, ground chick peas and black beans, and tamarind juice. Mix thoroughly and let simmer another 15 minutes.

4

Add lemon juice, coriander and coconut. Remove pan from heat and serve piping hot.

IMLI KA PAANI

Ripe Tamarind Sauce

Serves   6

Preparation time   10 minutes plus overnight soaking and chilling time

This sweet-and-sour chutney is often served as a decoration on yogurt-based savouries and *chaat* (salty snack) dishes; it also adds variety to taste. It can of course be served by itself as a side dish.

Imperial (Metric)	American
2 oz (50g) seedless ripe tamarind pulp	¼ cup seedless, ripe tamarind pulp
½ pint (300ml) water	1¼ cups water
Sea salt, to taste	Sea salt, to taste
1 tablespoonful raw cane sugar	1 tablespoon raw sugar
¼ teaspoonful freshly ground black pepper	¼ teaspoon freshly ground black pepper
½ teaspoonful chilli powder	½ teaspoon chili powder
½ teaspoonful white cumin seeds, dry roasted and freshly ground	½ teaspoon white cumin seeds, dry roasted and freshly ground
1 tablespoonful chopped mint leaves	1 tablespoon chopped mint leaves

1

Soak the tamarind pulp in measured water overnight. Then mash it into the water and blend thoroughly. Strain liquid in a sieve and discard fibres.

2

Stir in the rest of the ingredients, except for mint, and whisk thoroughly until sugar is fully dissolved.

3

Sprinkle with mint, and serve chilled.

Note: Ideally this sauce should neither be too thick nor too runny.

JAL ZEERA

Cumin Sauce

Serves 6
Preparation time   20 minutes plus chilling time

You may serve this as an appetizer before a main meal, although it is usually served stuffed into *golgappe* — a *chaat* dish.

Imperial (Metric)	American
3 oz (75g) tamarind pulp	⅓ cup tamarind pulp
1½ pints (900g) warm water	3¾ cups warm water
1 tablespoonful raw cane sugar	1 tablespoon raw sugar
Sea salt, to taste	Sea salt, to taste
12 fresh mint leaves, ground	12 fresh mint leaves, ground
1½ teaspoonsful white cumin seeds, dry roasted and ground	1½ teaspoons white cumin seeds, dry roasted and ground
1 teaspoonful chilli powder	1 teaspoon chili powder
1 teaspoonful fresh lemon juice	1 teaspoon fresh lemon juice

1

Soak the tamarind in the measured warm water about 15 minutes. Then mash it into the water and blend thoroughly. Strain liquid in a sieve and discard the fibres.

2

Add the rest of the ingredients one by one, in order of listing, and stir thoroughly.

3

Chill before serving; stir before each use.

PAALAK KA RAITA

Spinach Raita

Serves 4
Preparation time   10 minutes plus chilling time
Cooking time   10 minutes

A special lightweight raita that aids the digestion; a particular favourite of Popeye fans!

Imperial (Metric)	American
8 oz (225g) fresh spinach	4 cups fresh spinach
½ pint (300ml) natural yogurt	1¼ cups plain yogurt
Sea salt, to taste	Sea salt, to taste
1 green chilli, finely chopped	1 green chili pepper, finely chopped
1 tablespoonful ghee	1 tablespoon ghee
1 teaspoonful each: fenugreek, mustard and cumin seeds	1 teaspoon each: fenugreek, mustard and cumin seeds
1 teaspoonful chilli powder	1 teaspoon chili powder

1
Clean, wash and chop the spinach; then boil it. When cool, squeeze out the water.

2
Whisk yogurt, together with salt and green chilli, to a smooth consistency. Add spinach and blend thoroughly.

3
Heat ghee, together with seeds, to a high temperature. Then pour over yogurt mixture and stir well.

4
Sprinkle with chilli powder, chill, and serve.

MAKHAANE KA RAITA

Lotus Puff Raita

Serves 6
Preparation time 10 minutes plus chilling time
Cooking time 10 minutes

Light on the stomach and cool in effect, here is an exotic raita *par excellence*!

Imperial (Metric)	American
1½ teaspoonsful ghee	1½ teaspoons ghee
3 oz (75g) lotus puffs*, halved	3 oz lotus puffs*, halved
¾ pint (450ml) natural yogurt	2 cups plain yogurt
Sea salt, to taste	Sea salt, to taste
½ teaspoonful freshly ground black pepper	½ teaspoon freshly ground black pepper
1½ teaspoonsful each:	1½ teaspoons each:
flaked almonds (pre-soaked),	slivered almonds (presoaked)
flaked cashews (pre-soaked),	slivered cashews (presoaked)
White cumin seeds (roasted and ground)	White cumin seeds (roasted and ground)

*Roasted lotus seeds.

1

Heat the ghee in a *kadhai* or deep frying pan, and sauté lotus puffs until deep golden.

2

Beat yogurt together with salt and pepper to a smooth consistency. Add lotus puffs, almonds and cashews and blend thoroughly. Garnish with cumin and serve chilled.

GHIYA KA RAITA

Marrow (Squash) Raita

Serves 4
Preparation time   5 minutes plus chilling time
Cooking time   10 minutes

This low-calorie dish is sure to delight your digestive system. Serve with hot dishes to lessen the chilli effect.

Imperial (Metric)	American
4 oz (100g) grated marrow	¾ cup squash
8 fl oz (240ml) natural yogurt	1 cup plain yogurt
Sea salt, to taste	Sea salt, to taste
Pinch of asafoetida powder	Pinch of asafoetida powder
2 green chillies, chopped	2 green chili peppers, chopped
1 teaspoonsful white cumin seeds, roasted and ground	1 teaspoon white cumin seeds, roasted and ground
1 tablespooonful fresh mint, finely chopped	1 tablespoon fresh mint, finely chopped

1

Boil the marrow (squash). Then cool it and squeeze out the water.

2

Place the yogurt in a large bowl together with salt and whisk to a smooth consistency. Stir in the marrow (squash), asafoetida and green chillies, and blend thoroughly.

3

Garnish with cumin and mint. Serve chilled.

BHAANTE KA RAITA

Aubergine (Eggplant) Raita

Serves 6
Preparation time 10 minutes plus chilling time
Cooking time 5 minutes

This yogurt-based mixture, although unusual, is nevertheless delectable. You may substitute another preferred vegetable.

Imperial (Metric)	American
1 large aubergine	1 large eggplant
Ghee, to fry	Ghee, to fry
¾ pint (450ml) natural yogurt	2 cups plain yogurt
Sea salt, to taste	Sea salt, to taste
1½ teaspoonsful white cumin seeds, roasted and ground	1½ teaspoons white cumin seeds, roasted and ground
1 tablespoonful coriander leaves, finely chopped	1 tablespoon cilantro (coriander), finely chopped
1 teaspoonful chilli powder	1 teaspoon chili powder
½ teaspoonful mustard seeds, freshly ground	½ teaspoon mustard seeds,. freshly ground

1

Clean and wash the aubergine (eggplant); then slice into convenient-sized pieces.

2

Heat the ghee in a *kadhai* or frying pan. Fry the aubergine (eggplant) until golden, then drain on paper towels.

3

Beat yogurt with salt and cumin until smooth. Stir in coriander and blend thoroughly.

4

Stir the aubergine (eggplant) into yogurt and sprinkle with chilli and mustard powders. Serve chilled.

CHUKANDER KA SALAAD

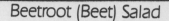

Beetroot (Beet) Salad

Serves 4
Preparation time 15 minutes

In India salads are treated as a side dish with a main meal; they are usually served instead of a chutney and to complement the pickles.

Imperial (Metric)	American
2 beetroots, cooked	2 beets, cooked
4 spring onions	4 scallions
2 green peppers	2 green peppers
½ medium-sized cucumber	½ medium-sized cucumber
1 green chilli	1 green chili pepper
Sea salt, to taste	Sea salt, to taste
1 tablespoonful fresh lemon juice	1 tablespoon fresh lemon juice
3 tablespoonsful coriander leaves	3 tablespoons cilantro (coriander)

1

Cut the beetroot (beets), spring onions (scallions), green peppers and cucumbers into round slices, and arrange on a serving dish.

2

Slice green chilli lengthways, and arrange it together with the green part of the spring onions (scallions) around the sliced ingredients.

3

Stir in salt and serve sprinkled with lemon juice and coriander.

MOOLI AUR SANTARE KA SALAAD

Radish and Satsuma Salad

Serves 4
Preparation time 15 minutes

You may experiment with alternative vegetables, varying texture and colour. This salad should prove popular with everyone!

Imperial (Metric)	American
1 large white radish (*mooli*)	1 large white radish (*mooli*)
1 seedless satsuma	1 seedless satsuma
4 firm, red tomatoes, cut into segments	4 firm red tomatoes, cut into segments
2 carrots	2 carrots
4 cauliflower florets	4 cauliflower florets
1 green chilli	1 green chili pepper
½ teaspoonful whole mustard seeds, crushed	½ teaspoon whole mustard seeds, crushed
Sea salt, to taste	Sea salt, to taste
½ teaspoonful freshly ground black pepper	½ teaspoon freshly ground black pepper
1 tablespoonful fresh lemon juice	1 tablespoon fresh lemon juice
2 tablespoonsful chopped coriander leaves	2 tablespoons chopped cilantro (coriander)

1

Slice the radish, satsuma, tomatoes, carrots, cauliflower and chilli into strips and rounds for visual variety, and arrange them on a serving dish.

2

Sprinkle mustard, salt and pepper over the mixture.

3

Sprinkle with lemon juice and serve garnished with coriander leaves.

NEEBU KA TELIA ACHAAR

Lemons Pickled in Oil

Serves 50 plus	
Preparation time 20 minutes plus 10 days pickling time	

This pickle adds zip to a meal and aids digestion; it is excellent when served with bland dishes like *dhals* and boiled rice.

Imperial (Metric)	American
12 juicy lemons	12 juicy lemons
1 tablespoonful carom seeds, whole	1 tablespoon carom seeds, whole
1 teaspoonful turmeric	1 teaspoon turmeric
3 tablespoonsful sea salt	3 tablespoons sea salt
½ teaspoonful asafoetida powder	½ teaspoon asafoetida powder
12 dry red chillies, whole	12 dried red chili peppers, whole
½ pint (300ml) mustard oil	1¼ cups mustard oil

1

Wash and dry the lemons and cut into 4 "petals" almost all the way through, but making sure that lemon pieces are not separated; remove pips.

2

Mix together carom seeds, turmeric, salt and asafoetida and, with the use of a little oil, prepare a thick mixture.

3

Stuff mixture into lemons and close "petals." Then place lemons and chillies in a clean, dry glass jar and drop in remaining spice mixture. Pour in the oil, adjusting the quantity so that the lemons and chillies are completely submerged.

4

Cover the mouth of the jar with a clean cloth, tie it with string to secure it, and leave it out in the sun, or alternatively in the warmest place in the house, until the lemon skin is tender — about 10 days. Shake the jar at least once a day.

Note: To decrease the pickling time, you may warm the oil before use.

AAM KA NONCHA

Mango Salt Mine

Serves	50 plus
Preparation time	15 minutes plus 1 week pickling time

This must certainly be the easiest pickle to make. Its taste will haunt you for a long time!

Imperial (Metric)	American
8 medium-sized green mangoes	8 medium-sized green mangoes
5 tablespoonsful sea salt	¼ cup sea salt
2 teaspoonsful cayenne pepper	2 teaspoons cayenne pepper
½ teaspoonful asafoetida powder	½ teaspoon asafoetida powder

1

Wash and peel the mangoes; cut into 8 pieces each and let dry. Stir in salt (reserve 1 tablespoon for later use), cayenne pepper and asafoetida and mix thoroughly.

2

Sprinkle the base of a clean, dry, lidded jar with the reserved salt and then drop in mango pieces. Shake well and cover jar.

3

Place jar outside in the sun until it matures — about a week. Alternatively, place it in the warmest place in the house. Shake the jar at least once a day and before each serving.

Note: One piece of pickled mango usually suffices for one person per meal. This pickle perks up the blandest of meals!

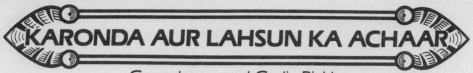

KARONDA AUR LAHSUN KA ACHAAR

Gooseberry and Garlic Pickle

Serves	*50 plus*
Preparation time	*20 minutes plus 2 weeks pickling time*

Here is a truly exotic pickle to titillate your taste buds; serve it to lend piquancy to your meal.

Imperial (Metric)	American
8 oz (225g) gooseberries	1½ cups gooseberries
10 cloves garlic	10 cloves garlic
Sea salt, to taste	Sea salt, to taste
½ teaspoonful asafoetida powder	½ teaspoon asafoetida powder
1 teaspoonful mustard seeds, coarsely ground	1 teaspoon mustard seeds, coarsely ground
1 teaspoonful cayenne pepper	1 teaspoon cayenne pepper
1 teaspoonful turmeric	1 teaspoon turmeric
Mustard oil, as necessary	Mustard oil, as necessary

1

Clean and wash the gooseberries and garlic and cut in half lengthways; remove seeds from gooseberries.

2

Rub about 1 teaspoon sea salt and half of the asafoetida powder thoroughly over the gooseberries and garlic. Stir in salt to taste together with the mustard, cayenne pepper and turmeric and blend well.

3

Take a clean, dry crock or glass jar. Sprinkle remaining asafoetida and ½ teaspoon salt on its base; then drop in spiced gooseberries and garlic. Add enough oil to half submerge the preparation. Stir thoroughly so that it is well-moistened.

4

Cover the mouth of the crock or jar with a clean cloth, tie with string to secure it, and put it outside in the sun (or the warmest place in the house) until the pickle is ready — about two weeks. Shake the jar at least once a day and before each serving.

BHARWAAN LAAL MIRCH KA ACHAAR

Stuffed Red Chilli Pickle

Serves 20 plus
Preparation time 30 minutes plus 10 days pickling time

This well-liked pickle will promote the appetite and enhance the flavour of food. It goes well with a main meal.

Imperial (Metric)	American
1 lb (450g) red chillies	1 pound red chili peppers
3 tablespoonsful each: mustard, coriander, fennel, fenugreek and nigella seeds	3 tablespoons each: mustard, coriander, fennel, fenugreek and nigella seeds
3 teaspoonsful each: green mango powder and turmeric	3 teaspoons each: green mango powder and turmeric
3 tablespoonsful sea salt	3 tablespoons sea salt
¼ pint (150ml) mustard oil	⅔ cup mustard oil

1

Clean, wash and dry the chillies and slit in the middle, lengthways.

2

Dry roast and coarsely grind the seeds and add green mango and turmeric powders. Stir in salt (reserve 1 teaspoon for later use), and add enough oil to make a pliable mixture.

3

Stuff the mixture into chillies.

4

Take a clean, dry jar and sprinkle reserved salt on its base. Then drop in chillies and pour the oil over them. Turn chillies over carefully so that oil moistens them all.

5

Cover jar, and put it in the sun (or the warmest place in the house) until the pickle is ready — about 10 days.

Note: You may use warmed oil to decrease the pickling time.

CHATPATA ACHAAR

Orange and Lemon Sweet Pickle

Serves 40 plus
Preparation time 20 minutes plus 1 week pickling time
Cooking time 25 minutes

This tangy pickle is scrumptious and livens up the taste buds.

Imperial (Metric)	American
8 oz (225g) raw cane sugar	1⅓ cups raw sugar
1 tablespoonful sea salt	1 tablespoon sea salt
1½ teaspoonsful chilli powder	1½ teaspoons chili powder
1 tablespoonful crushed	1 tablespoon crushed
coriander seeds	coriander seeds
2 teaspoonsful fennel seeds,	2 teaspoons fennel seeds,
coarsely ground	coarsely ground
1 pint (600ml) water	2½ cups water
10 each: juicy oranges and lemons	10 each juicy oranges and lemons

1

Place the sugar, salt, chilli powder, coriander, fennel and water in a saucepan, and boil over medium heat about 15 minutes. Lower heat and cook another 10 minutes. Remove pan from the heat and let it cool.

2

Meanwhile wash, clean, and dry the oranges and lemons, and cut into 8 pieces each; remove pips and top flesh, leaving outer skin and a thick layer of flesh.

3

Take a clean, dry crock or glass jar. Drop in the oranges and lemons and then the cooked mixture. Cover crock, and shake thoroughly. Then place it in the sun (or the warmest place in the house) until fruit skins are tender — about a week.

4

Shake the jar once a day and before each use.

GOBHI KA MEETHA ACHAAR

Cauliflower Sweet Pickle

Serves	30 plus
Preparation time	10 minutes plus 1 week pickling time
Cooking time	25 minutes

This is an ideal sweet pickle for the adventurous; plenty of room for experimentation with different vegetables!

Imperial (Metric)	American
Water, as necessary	Water, as necessary
2 lb (900g) cauliflower florets	2 pounds cauliflower florets
1 (2-in/5cm) piece of fresh root ginger, sliced	1 (2-in) piece of fresh ginger root, sliced
4 large cloves of garlic, quartered	4 large cloves of garlic, quartered
1 tablespoonful sea salt	1 tablespoon sea salt
1 teaspoonful each: cayenne pepper and turmeric	1 teaspoon each: cayenne pepper and turmeric
1 teaspoonful each: black cumin and mustard seeds	1 teaspoon each: black cumin and mustard seeds
8 oz (225g) jaggery (unrefined palm sugar)	1 cup jaggery (unrefined palm sugar)
5 tablespoonsful wine vinegar	1/3 cup wine vinegar

1

Half-fill a deep saucepan with water and bring to a boil over medium heat. Drop in the cauliflower, ginger and garlic and remove pan from heat immediately. Drain and let cool.

2

Dry cauliflower, ginger and garlic and place in a large glass jar. Stir in salt, cayenne pepper, turmeric, cumin and mustard. Blend thoroughly by shaking the jar.

3

In a separate saucepan place the sugar and vinegar and bring to a boil. Pour over the cauliflower mixture, shake the jar, and stand it in the sun (or the warmest place in the house) for about a week.

AAM KA MEETHA ACHAAR

Sweet Mango Pickle

Serves 20
Preparation time 15 minutes
Cooking time 30 minutes

This sweet pickle should find favour with young and old alike; it tastes delicious.

Imperial (Metric)	American
1 lb (450g) green mangoes	1 pound green mangoes
2 teaspoonsful sea salt	2 teaspoons sea salt
1½ lb (675g) jaggery (unrefined palm sugar)	3 cups jaggery (unrefined palm sugar)
1 teaspoonful chilli powder	1 teaspoon chili powder
½ teaspoonful nigella seeds	½ teaspoon nigella seeds
A large pinch of turmeric and asafoetida powders	A large pinch of turmeric and asafoetida powders

1

Wash, dry, peel and shred the mangoes. Stir in salt and blend well.

2

Place salted mangoes in a deep pan, add jaggery, and place over medium heat; stir continuously.

3

When the mixture takes on a thick and smooth consistency — after approximately 15 minutes — lower heat. Blend in the rest of the ingredients and stir vigorously. After 2 minutes, remove pan from heat and let mixture cool.

4

Store in a suitable container and serve as desired.

Chapter 9

Mashhoor Namkeen Pakwaan
Sensational Savouries

Indian cuisine possesses an inexhaustible stock of snack and "munch" dishes — some of them are sensational and are known the world over. *Samosas* and *pakodas* are not only well-known in the West, they command a large following among the young and old there! But these are only two out of thousands and thousands of savouries made throughout India. Regional variations and specialities in this area, as in others, are pronounced — main ingredients are different; the medium of cooking differs; and methods and timings of cooking the same dish are vastly different, too. Some of these dishes are offered on the following pages.

The making of these dishes is often quick and easy. Like most Indian dishes, snacks offer a lot of room for experimentation for the adventurous. Many Indian snacks are suitable for picnics and parties; they go down well with drinks, too.

A little bit of imagination can do wonders for your dishes, so do pay close attention to presentation. As many of these dishes are served on their own, they must look appetizing. Garnishing goes a long way toward achieving this: use coriander leaves and tomato, onion and lemon slices or green chillies; they add a lot of colour to your dishes. Attractive-looking savouries are sure to make your guests peckish, and make their mouths water!

SAMOSA KHOL

Pastry Dough

Serves 4
Preparation time 15 minutes plus resting time

This is the basic recipe for making the dough for the world-renowned *samosa* dish. The filling — made in many ways and with different ingredients — changes the *samosa*'s name and taste; the principle of making the outer covering remains the same.

Imperial (Metric)	American
3 tablespoonsful ghee	3 tablespoons ghee
4 oz (100g) wholemeal flour	1 cup whole wheat flour
Pinch of sea salt	Pinch of sea salt
Pinch of baking powder	Pinch of baking powder
Water, as necessary	Water, as necessary

1

Rub the ghee into the flour; stir in salt and baking powder and continue rubbing the mixture until it assumes a crumbly texture. Gradually add water as necessary and knead into a stiff, but pliable, dough.

2

Divide dough into 4 portions. (Adjust the amount of flour and dough depending on the size and number of samosas required.) Flatten each portion by hand and then roll out into a thin, round disc.

3

Each disc should, in turn, be cut in half; thus a total of 8 half-moon shapes of pastry will be produced.

4

Cover the half-moons with a damp cloth and let them rest while the filling is being prepared.

GOBHI SAMOSA

Cauliflower Pastry

Serves	4
Preparation time	15 minutes
Cooking time	25 minutes

This *samosa* has a vegetable filling; substitute another vegetable or perhaps use a mixture of them, if you wish. It goes down well with tea or drinks.

Imperial (Metric)	American
Ghee, as necessary	Ghee, as necessary
1 teaspoonful white cumin seeds	1 teaspoon white cumin seeds
1 tablespoonful chopped onion	1 tablespoon chopped onion
4 tablespoonsful grated cauliflower	4 tablespoons grated cauliflower
1 tablespoonful green peas	1 tablespoon green peas
Pinch of asafoetida powder	Pinch of asafoetida power
1 teaspoonful green mango powder	1 teaspoon green mango powder
Pinch of garam masala	Pinch of garam masala
½ teaspoonful sea salt (or to taste)	½ teaspoon sea salt (or to taste)
½ teaspoonful cayenne pepper	½ teaspoon cayenne pepper
8 pastry half-moons	8 pastry half-moons
Milk, to bind	Milk, to bind

1

Heat 1 tablespoon ghee in a *kadhai*, or a deep frying pan, and sauté the cumin until golden.

2

Add onion, cauliflower and peas and give it a good stir. Mix in asafoetida and mango powders, garam masala, salt and cayenne pepper, cover the pan, and cook over moderate heat for 10 minutes. Remove pan from heat and let filling cool.

3

Take one half-moon of pastry, brush its edges with milk, and fold into a cone. Fill it with one-eighth of the cooked mixture and seal the top. Make the other samosas in the same way.

4

Heat sufficient ghee in a *kadhai* and deep-fry the samosas — 4 at a time — over low heat. When golden, remove and place on paper towels.

5

Serve hot or cold, with or without a chutney.

MOONG SAMOSA

Mung Bean Pastry

Serves	4
Preparation time	20 minutes
Cooking time	25 minutes

Samosas can be eaten hot or cold; their filling can be made to suit your palate. You can also serve them as a side dish with a meal, or as a *chaat* (savoury snack) dish!

Imperial (Metric)	American
Ghee, as necessary	Ghee, as necessary
1 tablespoonful chopped onion	1 tablespoon chopped onion
Pinch of asafoetida powder	Pinch of asafoetida powder
1 teaspoonful mustard seeds	1 teaspoon mustard seeds
½ teaspoonful grated fresh root ginger	½ teaspoon grated, fresh ginger root
Pinch each: garam masala and green mango powder	Pinch each: garam masala and green mango powder
½ teaspoonful sea salt (or to taste)	½ teaspoon sea salt (or to taste)
½ teaspoonful cayenne pepper	½ teaspoon cayenne pepper
4 tablespoonsful skinless split mung beans (pre-soaked)	4 tablespoons skinless split mung beans (presoaked)
1 tablespoonful shredded coriander leaves	1 tablespoon shredded cilantro (coriander)
8 pastry half-moons	8 pastry half-moons
Water, to bind	Water, to bind

1

Heat 2 teaspoons ghee in a *kadhai* or a deep frying pan over low heat. Sauté the onion, asafoetida powder, mustard and ginger until the onion is golden. Stir in garam masala, green mango powder, salt and cayenne pepper, and mix thoroughly.

2

Add the beans, cover pan, and cook over moderate heat for 10 minutes, until beans are tender. Stir in coriander, remove pan from heat, and you have the filling!

3

Take one half-moon of pastry, brush its edges with a little water, and fold into a triangular cone. Fill with 2 teaspoons of the cooled mixture and seal the top. Make the other triangles similarly.

4

Heat sufficient ghee in a *kadhai* or a deep fryer. Deep-fry the *samosas* over a low heat until golden all over; cook 4 at a time. Remove when cooked and drain on paper towels.

PANEER KE PAKODE

Cream Cheese Fritters

Serves	*4*

Preparation time   10 minutes plus 20 minutes standing time

Cooking time   15 minutes

Use homemade cream cheese to make these snacks; the batter may also be made with chick pea flour. They are a good accompaniment to tea or drinks.

Imperial (Metric)	American
4 oz (100g) wholemeal flour	1 cup whole wheat flour
¼ pint (150ml) water	⅔ cup water
½ teaspoon sea salt (or to taste)	½ teaspoon sea salt (or to taste)
½ teaspoon cayenne pepper	½ teaspoon cayenne pepper
Pinch each: garam masala and	Pinch each: garam masala and
green mango powder	green mango powder
4 oz (100g) cream cheese,	¼ cup cream cheese,
cut into pieces	cut into pieces
Ghee, for deep-frying	Ghee, for deep-frying

1

Place the flour in a deep bowl. Gradually add water to make a batter of smooth consistency. Add salt, cayenne pepper and the spice powders, and whisk thoroughly. Then let it stand about 20 minutes.

2

Heat sufficient ghee in a *kadhai* or a deep fryer. Pick up the pieces of cheese — one at a time — completely coat with the batter and carefully slide each into the sizzling ghee. Cook a few *pakodas* at a time until golden all over. Remove from heat and drain on paper towels.

3

Serve hot with a chutney of your choice.

GOBHI KE PAKODE

Cauliflower Fritters

Serves 4
Preparation time   10 minutes plus 20 minutes standing time
Cooking time   20 minutes

Indian *pakodas* are very well-known and liked in the West. This particular type of dish can be made with almost any vegetable of your choice. Serve as a snack. It tastes particularly nice with a mint or mango chutney.

Imperial (Metric)	American
4 oz (100g) chick pea flour	1 cup chick pea flour
Water, as required	Water, as required
Sea salt, as necessary	Sea salt, as necessary
½ teaspoonful cayenne pepper	½ teaspoon cayenne pepper
1 tablespoonful dried pomegranate seeds, crushed	1 tablespoon dried pomegranate seeds, crushed
8 oz (225g) small cauliflower florets	2¼ cups small cauliflower florets
Ghee, for deep-frying	Ghee, for deep frying

1

Place the flour in a deep bowl. Gradually add water and make a medium-thick batter of smooth consistency. (Thin batter produces crisp *pakodas*, whereas thick batter produces sumptuous ones; adjust the amount of water according to how you like your *pakodas*.)

2

Stir in ½ teaspoon salt, cayenne pepper and pomegranate seeds, and whisk thoroughly. Then let stand about 20 minutes.

3

Boil 1 pint/2½ cups water; add a pinch of sea salt. Drop cauliflower florets into the water. Remove pan from heat after 2 minutes. Drain off the water, and place the florets on a flat dish.

4

Heat sufficient ghee in a *kadhai* or a deep fryer. Dip each floret well into the batter to coat it, and slide into the sizzling ghee; deep-fry over moderate heat until *pakodas* are deep golden. Cook 3 or 4 *pakodas* at a time. When cooked, remove and place on paper towels to drain.

5

Serve hot with a preferred chutney.

DABAL ROTI ALOO KE TIKKE

Bread and Potato Cutlets

Serves 6
Preparation time   15 minutes
Cooking time   20 minutes

This delicious savoury dish serves not only as a snack, but can be served as a side dish with a main meal, too. Adjust quantities of chilli and salt to your liking.

Imperial (Metric)	*American*
6 thick slices of wholemeal bread	6 thick slices of whole wheat bread
3 large potatoes, boiled, peeled and mashed	3 large potatoes, boiled, peeled and mashed
1 tablespoonful chopped coriander leaves	1 tablespoon chopped cilantro (coriander)
½ teaspoonful green mango powder	½ teaspoon green mango powder
1 green chilli, chopped	1 green chili pepper, chopped
1 medium-sized onion, finely chopped	1 medium-sized onion, minced
1 teaspoonful sea salt (or to taste)	1 teaspoon sea salt (or to taste)
Vegetable oil, for shallow-frying	Vegetable oil, for shallow-frying

1

Soak the bread in water for a couple of minutes and then squeeze out the water. Place the bread in a bowl, add potato, coriander, mango powder, chilli, onion and salt, and make a pliable dough.

2

Divide the dough into 12 portions. Grease your palms and make a small fat disc from each portion by hand.

3

Heat 1 tablespoon oil on a griddle, and shallow-fry four discs over moderate heat until nice and brown on both sides, adding more oil as necessary. Cook remaining discs similarly.

4

Serve hot with a preferred chutney.

KELE KE KABAB

Banana (Plantain) Croquettes

Serves 6
Preparation time 10 minutes
Cooking time 25 minutes

A delightful snack dish which pleases people of all culinary persuasions. It has an exotic taste and is open to experimentation.

Imperial (Metric)	American
4 green bananas (plantains)	4 plantains
2 large potatoes	2 large potatoes
1 small onion, finely chopped	1 small onion, finely chopped
Pinch of grated, fresh ginger root	Pinch of grated, fresh ginger root
2 green chillies, crushed	2 green chilies, crushed
1 tablespoonful shredded coriander leaves	1 tablespoon shredded cilantro (coriander)
1 teaspoonful sea salt (or to taste)	1 teaspoon sea salt (or to taste)
1 teaspoonful green mango powder	1 teaspoon green mango powder
Chick pea flour, to bind	Chick pea flour, to bind
Wholemeal breadcrumbs, to coat	Whole wheat breadcrumbs, to coat
Ghee, for shallow-frying	Ghee, for shallow-frying

1

Boil the bananas (plantain) and potatoes in water; peel and mash them.

2

Add the onion, ginger, chillies, coriander, salt and mango powder, and mix thoroughly. Stir in chick pea flour as necessary and make into a pliable dough.

3

Pluck 12 small balls from the dough and mould them by hand into thick, round discs.

4

Place the breadcrumbs in a shallow dish and keep it handy.

5

Heat a griddle and brush with 1 tablespoon ghee. Roll each disc in the breadcrumbs and shallow-fry, over moderate heat — cook 4 at a time. Turn them over from time to time until nice and brown on both sides; add more ghee as necessary.

6

Serve hot straight from the griddle with a chutney of your choice.

KAMAL KAKDI KI TIKKI

Lotus Stem Cutlets

Serves	6
Preparation time	10 minutes
Cooking time	25 minutes

This exotic cutlet is truly exciting in taste once you have put together all the ingredients. Serve as a snack or as a side dish.

Imperial (Metric)	American
8 oz (225g) lotus stems, broken, scraped and boiled	½ pound lotus stems, broken, scraped and boiled
4 oz (100g) chick pea flour	1 cup chick pea flour
3 tablespoonsful natural yogurt	3 tablespoons plain yogurt
1 teaspoonful sea salt	1 teaspoon sea salt
1 green chilli, chopped	1 green chili pepper, chopped
1 tablespoonful chopped coriander leaves	1 tablespoon chopped cilantro (coriander)
1 teaspoonful garam masala	1 teaspoon garam masala
Ghee, as necessary	Ghee, as necessary

1

Grind the lotus stems finely over a *sil-batta*. Then add the rest of the ingredients, except for the ghee. Blend thoroughly and make into a dough.

2

Divide the dough into 12 portions and form into small, fat discs.

3

Place a griddle over moderate heat, add 1 tablespoon ghee, and position 4 discs on it. Shallow-fry on both sides until brown all over, adding more ghee as necessary. Cook the remaining discs in the same way.

4

Serve hot with a chutney of your choice.

MASAALEDAAR KABAB

Spicy Hot Dogs

Serves	4
Preparation time	10 minutes
Cooking time	20 minutes

These snacks will give you inner warmth; you can make a meal out of them! Make the mixture and shape in advance; cook just before serving, and impress everyone with your culinary dexterity!

Imperial (Metric)	American
4 large potatoes	4 large potatoes
½ small onion, finely chopped	½ small onion, minced
½ teaspoonful grated fresh root ginger	½ teaspoon grated, fresh ginger root
2 green chillies, crushed	2 green chili peppers, crushed
½ teaspoonful garam masala	½ teaspoon garam masala
½ teaspoonful sea salt (or to taste)	½ teaspoon sea salt (or to taste)
1 tablespoonful chopped coriander leaves	1 tablespoon chopped cilantro (coriander)
1 tablespoonful lemon juice	1 tablespoon lemon juice
3 tablespoonsful chick pea flour	3 tablespoons chick pea flour
Water, as necessary	Water, as necessary
Vegetable oil, for deep-frying	Vegetable oil, for deep-frying

1
Boil the potatoes in water, then peel and mash them.

2
Place the mashed potato in a bowl; add the onion, ginger, chillies, garam masala, salt and coriander and mix thoroughly. Add lemon juice and mix again.

3
Mould the mixture into 8 (or more) sausage shapes.

4
Put chick pea flour in a deep bowl; gradually add water as necessary to make a very thin batter. Keep it handy.

5
Heat sufficient oil in a *kadhai* or a deep frying pan. Dip each "sausage" into the batter and deep-fry — 4 at a time — over moderate heat until deep golden all over.

6
Serve hot with whatever you fancy!

NAMKEEN KHURME

Flour Diamonds

Serves	6
Preparation time	15 minutes
Cooking time	15 minutes

This snack dish is suitable for all occasions! Serve with tea or drinks; take it out on picnics, or eat between meals.

Imperial (Metric)	American
6 oz (175g) wholemeal flour	1½ cups whole wheat flour
4 tablespoonsful ghee	4 tablespoons ghee
Sea salt, to taste	Sea salt, to taste
6 black peppercorns, coarsely ground	6 black peppercorns, coarsely ground
Pinch of carom seeds	Pinch of carom seeds
Tepid water, as necessary	Tepid water, as necessary
Vegetable oil, for deep-frying	Vegetable oil, for deep-frying

1

Place the flour, ghee, salt, pepper and carom seeds in a bowl; rub together and, with spoonsful of tepid water as necessary, knead into a stiff dough. Mould the dough into a ball and roll it out into a large, thin, round disc. With a sharp knife, make diamond shapes of the desired size.

2

Heat sufficient oil in a *kadhai* or a deep fryer to smoking point; reduce heat to low and deep-fry the diamonds until golden all over. Remove, and drain excess oil on paper towels.

3

Serve hot or cold. Store in an airtight container; do not leave it in the open for long periods.

DHOKHA — RASAAJ

Savoury Slices

Serves	6
Preparation time	10 minutes
Cooking time	25 minutes

This delightful tea-time savoury is a particular favourite of the Pandya family. It is versatile in that it can be served as a snack as well as a side dish; if you have ready gravy (page 28), this dish can be instantly converted into a curry, too!

Imperial (Metric)	American
12 oz (350g) chick pea flour	3 cups chick pea flour
½ pint (300ml) water	1¼ cups water
Mustard oil, as necessary	Mustard oil, as necessary
Pinch of garlic powder	Pinch of garlic powder
1 teaspoonful garam masala	1 teaspoon garam masala
2 teaspoonsful green mango powder	2 teaspoons green mango powder
2 green chillies, finely chopped	2 green chili peppers, minced
1½ teaspoonsful sea salt (or to taste)	1½ teaspoons sea salt (or to taste)
3 tablespoonsful coriander leaves, crushed	3 tablespoons cilantro, (coriander) crushed
small pinch of asafoetida powder	Small pinch of asafoetida powder

1

Place the flour and water in a deep bowl and whisk thoroughly into a batter of smooth consistency.

2

Heat 1 tablespoon oil in a saucepan. Add the batter and cook over moderate heat, stirring constantly.

3

Stir in the remaining ingredients, one by one, and blend thoroughly. When the liquid thickens into a dough, remove pan from heat and let it cool.

4

Mould the dough into a big sausage; then cut into thick, round slices.

5

Heat sufficient oil in a *kadhai*, or a deep fryer, and deep-fry the slices over low heat until deep golden. Remove and drain on paper towels.

6

Serve hot, with or without a chutney or pickle.

URAD DHALMOTH

Fried Black Beans

Serves 20
Preparation time   10 minutes plus overnight soaking
Cooking time   10 minutes

This crunchy snack dish is usually cooked and stored in advance. Serve with tea or drinks; suitable for picnics and parties, too!

Imperial (Metric)	American
1 lb (450g) skinless split black beans	2 cups skinless, split black beans
Mustard oil, for deep-frying	Mustard oil, for deep-frying
Sea salt, to taste	Sea salt, to taste
½ teaspoonful pounded red chillies	½ teaspoon pounded red chili peppers
Pinch of roasted ground cumin	Pinch of roasted ground cumin
1 teaspoonful green mango powder	1 teaspoon green mango powder
1 tablespoonful coarsely ground mustard seeds	1 tablespoon coarsely ground mustard seeds

1

Wash and soak the black beans in water overnight. Drain off the water and let the beans dry completely.

2

Heat sufficient oil in a *kadhai* or a deep frying pan to smoking point. Drop the beans, a little at a time, in the sizzling oil. Bubbles will form immediately on the surface; when the bubbles disappear — under a minute — remove the beans with a slotted spoon and drain on paper towels.

3

When cool, transfer to a large plate. Stir in the rest of the ingredients, one by one, and mix thoroughly.

4

Store in a suitable covered container and serve as required; do not leave the container open for too long. Shake the container before each use.

Chapter 10

Vishesh Chatpate Pakwaan
Special Savouries

Indian cuisine is full of pockets of specialities — some take generations to perfect; others can be learned rather more quickly. In this section of the book I would like to talk about a particular area and type of dishes that are special to me; I hope that you will come to love them, too, and they are relatively easy to cook.

The dishes that follow form two distinct groups: the Southern Indian snacks and the *Chaat* dishes. Some Southern Indian dishes are already known and popular in the West, like *dosa*. Others are gaining popularity steadily. One reason for this phenomenon could be that these preparations from the South are singularly ungreasy. The main ingredients used in making these dishes are coconut, dried beans, tamarind and rice. This you will no doubt witness in most dishes originating from that region. These dishes are usually served hot.

Chaat shops sell *chaat* dishes in many parts of India and the addiction of people to these savouries is an interesting aspect of Indian social life. Like people flocking around wine bars and pubs in the West, Indians make a bee-line to these tiny shops and kiosks every afternoon. There are no age restrictions and these dishes are cheap to buy, and tasty, too. A *chaat* shop is well stocked, in addition to the main goodies, with the *chaat* spices which include salt (sea salt, black salt), roasted and ground cumin, pounded red chillies and garam masala; also in evidence are the *chaat* sauces — a tamarind or mango sauce and plain yogurt whisked in a little water. Most *chaat* dishes are served cold; they are cooked during the day and served in the afternoon while they are still fresh.

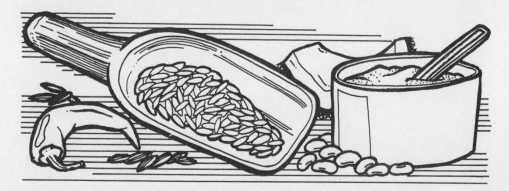

MEDHU WADA

Black Bean Dumplings

Serves 6
Preparation time   10 minutes plus overnight soaking
Cooking time   25 minutes

This is a truly versatile dish. As a Southern Indian delicacy it is served with coconut chutney and *saambhar* sauce; it can also be served as a dry or wet snack or as a side dish with a main meal.

Imperial (Metric)	American
8 oz (225g) dried black beans	1 cup dried black beans
Pinch of asafoetida powder	Pinch of asafoetida powder
2 green chillies, finely chopped	2 green chili peppers, finely chopped
1 teaspoonful ground fennel	1 teaspoon ground fennel
6 curry leaves, chopped	6 curry leaves, chopped
Sea salt, to taste	Sea salt, to taste
Water, as necessary	Water, as necessary
Ghee, for deep-frying	Ghee, for deep-frying

1

Wash the beans in several changes of water and then soak them overnight. Drain off the water, and grind over a *sil-batta* (or an electric grinder).

2

Add the asafoetida powder, chillies, fennel, curry leaves and salt to the ground beans and, adding water as necessary, make a thick paste.

3

Grease a clean plastic sheet with a little ghee and drop one tablespoon bean paste on it. Using wet fingers, mould the paste into a small, fat, round shape; make a hole in the middle like a doughnut. Use up the rest of the paste making similar shapes.

4

Heat sufficient ghee in a *kadhai* or a deep fryer, and cook a few of these *wadas* at a time. Remove when deep golden on both sides, and place on paper towels.

5

Serve hot or cold as the mood takes you!

SAADA DOSA

Plain Dosa

Serves 4
Preparation time 10 minutes plus overnight soaking
Cooking time 10 minutes

This Southern Indian delicacy serves as a light meal in itself; it is usually accompanied by coconut chutney and *saambhar* sauce.

Imperial (Metric)	American
4 oz (100g) brown rice	½ cup brown rice
4 oz (100g) dried black beans	½ cup dried black beans
1 teaspoonful ground cumin	1 teaspoon ground cumin
Pinch of asafoetida powder	Pinch of asafoetida powder
Sea salt, to taste	Sea salt, to taste
Vegetable oil, for frying	Vegetable oil, for frying
Accompanying sauces	Accompanying sauces

1

Wash and soak the rice and beans overnight.

2

Liquidize them in a blender to a thin batter of pouring consistency. Add the cumin, asafoetida and salt and whisk again. Let stand until you are ready to cook the *dosas*.

3

Place a griddle or frying pan over medium heat. When quite hot, add 1 teaspoon oil. Then pour 1 tablespoon batter on the griddle and quickly spread the mixture around. Turn it over with a spatula and cook on the other side, making sure you do not burn it.

4

Serve straight from the griddle with coconut chutney and *saambhar*.

BHARWAAN DOSA

Vegetarian Dosa

Serves	4
Preparation time	10 minutes
Cooking time	20 minutes

Like most Southern Indian dishes, *dosa* is an ungreasy preparation. The stuffing in a *dosa* can be of many types; this one is an example of the vegetarian variety.

Imperial (Metric)	American
2 large potatoes	2 large potatoes
2 teaspoonsful ghee	2 teaspoons ghee
1 small onion, finely chopped	1 small onion, minced
Pinch of turmeric	Pinch of turmeric
Sea salt, to taste	Sea salt, to taste
Pinch of cayenne pepper	Pinch of cayenne pepper
4 curry leaves	4 curry leaves
½ teaspoonful green mango powder	½ teaspoon green mango powder
4 plain *dosas* (see previous recipe)	4 plain *dosas* (see previous recipe)
Accompanying sauces	Accompanying sauces

1

Boil the potatoes. Then peel and dice them.

2

Heat the ghee in a *kadhai* or a saucepan and sauté the onion until golden. Add the potato and stir a few times. Add turmeric, salt, cayenne pepper and curry leaves, and blend well. Sprinkle with mango powder, and add a couple of spoons of water. Cover pan, lower heat, and cook about 5 minutes.

3

Make a plain dosa. While still on the griddle, place one-fourth of the potato mixture in a straight line down the middle; fold in the sides of the *dosa* to cover the filling. Make the remaining *dosas* in the same way.

4

Serve straight from the griddle with coconut chutney and *saambhar* sauce.

DHAL AUR CHAAWAL IDLI

Bean-Rice Cakes

Serves 4	
Preparation time 15 minutes plus overnight rising time	
Cooking time 15 minutes	

This is a Southern Indian tea-time snack; it also serves as a light meal by itself.

Imperial (Metric)	American
2 oz (50g) dried black beans, ground	½ cup dried black beans, ground
2 oz (50g) brown rice, ground	¼ cup brown rice, ground
½ teaspoonful sea salt (or to taste)	½ teaspoon sea salt (or to taste)
Pinch of baking powder	Pinch of baking powder
Water, as necessary	Water, as necessary
Ghee, for greasing	Ghee, for greasing
Chutneys to accompany	Chutneys to accompany

1

Place the ground beans and rice in a deep bowl and rub in the salt and baking powder. Add water as necessary to make a batter of "drop" consistency.

2

Leave the mixture in a warm place overnight. By the morning it should have doubled its original volume.

3

Take several small stainless steel bowls, grease them with ghee, and pour 4 teaspoons batter into each (or until they are three-quarters full).

4

Put these bowls into a suitable pan, and steam 10 to 12 minutes, or until firm. (If a cocktail stick (toothpick) inserted in the centre comes out clean, the *idlis* are ready.)

5

Serve hot with coconut chutney, *saambhar* or perhaps seasoned plain yogurt.

NAARIYAL IDLI

Coconut Crumpets

Serves 4

Preparation time   10 minutes plus overnight rising time

Cooking time   10 minutes

This is a delightfully ungreasy snack; serve it at tea-time. It is not very heavy on the stomach.

Imperial (Metric)	American
5 tablespoonsful grated fresh coconut	5 tablespoons grated, fresh coconut
3 tablespoonsful pigeon peas and black beans	3 tablespoons pigeon peas and black beans
8 oz (225g) brown rice, cooked	1 cup brown rice, cooked
2 green chillies, chopped	2 green chili peppers, chopped
1 tablespoonful chopped coriander leaves	1 tablespoon chopped cilantro (coriander)
¼ teaspoonful dry mustard	¼ teaspoon dry mustard
Pinch of baking powder	Pinch of baking powder
Coconut milk, as necessary	Coconut milk, as necessary
Ghee, for greasing	Ghee, for greasing
Seasoned natural yogurt, to serve	Seasoned plain yogurt, to serve

1

Grind the coconut, peas, beans, rice, chillies, coriander and mustard over a *sil-batta* (or use an electric grinder).

2

Stir in the baking powder and, adding coconut milk as necessary, make a thick batter. Place it in a warm place overnight to rise.

3

Take several small stainless steel bowls, grease with ghee, and fill three-quarters full with batter. Then put these bowls in a suitable pan and steam 10 minutes or so until the *idlis* are firm. (If a cocktail stick (toothpick) inserted in the centre comes out clean, the *idlis* are ready.)

4

Serve hot with seasoned yogurt.

ALOO UPMA

Potato Porridge

Serves	4
Preparation time	10 minutes
Cooking time	30 minutes

This is a unique offering from Southern India; it is something like an exotic and spiced porridge, to be eaten with a spoon.

Imperial (Metric)	American
4 medium-sized potatoes	4 medium-sized potatoes
2 teaspoonsful ghee	2 teaspoons ghee
½ teaspoonful mustard seeds	½ teaspoon mustard seeds
Pinch of asafoetida powder	Pinch of asafoetida powder
1 tablespoonful chopped onion	1 tablespoon chopped onion
1 tablespoonful mixed *dhal* powders	1 tablespoon mixed *dhal* powders
Sea salt, to taste	Sea salt, to taste
¼ pint (150ml) coconut milk	⅔ cup coconut milk
1 teaspoonful tamarind juice	1 teaspoon tamarind juice
1 green chilli, chopped	1 green chili pepper, chopped
1 tablespoonful chopped coriander leaves	1 tablespoon chopped cilantro (coriander)

1

Boil the potatoes; then peel and dice them.

2

Heat the ghee in a *kadhai* or a saucepan and sauté mustard seeds, asafoetida powder and onion 2 minutes.

3

Add the *dhal* powders, and stir a few times. Mix in the potatoes and salt, pour in the coconut milk, and cook over medium heat about 10 minutes.

4

Add the tamarind juice and chilli and blend well. Lower heat, cover pan, and cook another 10 minutes.

5

Sprinkle with chopped coriander and serve hot.

BHUTTA UPMA

Corn Porridge

Serves	4
Preparation time	10 minutes
Cooking time	20 minutes

This savoury dish is an interesting one in taste and appearance; it also offers scope for experimentation with alternative ingredients.

Imperial (Metric)	American
1 tablespoonful ghee	1 tablespoon ghee
1 tablespoonful chopped onion	1 tablespoon chopped onion
½ teaspoonful white cumin seeds	½ teaspoon white cumin seeds
Pinch of turmeric	Pinch of turmeric
2 oz (50g) wholemeal flour	½ cup whole wheat flour
4 oz (100g) maize meal	¾ cup cornmeal
¼ pint (150ml) buttermilk	⅔ cup buttermilk
Sea salt, to taste	Sea salt, to taste
1 green chilli, chopped	1 green chili pepper, chopped
3 tablespoonsful chopped coriander leaves	3 tablespoons chopped cilantro (coriander)

1

Heat the ghee in a *kadhai* or saucepan and sauté the onion until golden. Add the cumin and stir a few times before adding turmeric.

2

Mix in the flour, and stir constantly for about 5 minutes. Then stir in the maizemeal (cornmeal) and cook for another 5 minutes.

3

Pour in the buttermilk; add salt and chilli and stir well. Cover pan and simmer for 10 minutes, or until the mixture has no liquid left.

4

Serve hot, sprinkled with coriander.

MATAR KI CHAAT

Dried Whole Peas

Serves 4	
Preparation time 5 minutes plus 2 hours soaking time	
Cooking time 20 minutes	

A good *chaat* shop will have this dish on a large metal platter, over a low flame, on one side, while the other side has potato cutlets sizzling over a griddle. This tasty concoction is one of the main dishes of the Indian *chaat* repertoire.

Imperial (Metric)	American
4 oz (100g) dried whole peas	1 cup dried whole peas
Water, as necessary	Water, as necessary
Pinch of baking powder	Pinch of baking powder
Tamarind sauce	Tamarind sauce
Yogurt, whisked with water, to serve	Yogurt, whisked with water, to serve
Salt and *chaat* spices, to serve	Salt and *chaat* spices, to serve

1

Wash the peas in many changes of water, and then soak at least 2 hours.

2

Place the peas and enough fresh water to cover them in a saucepan and bring to a boil. Reduce heat and simmer about 10 minutes.

3

Stir in baking powder, cover pan, and cook for another 10 minutes, or until peas are soft. Drain off any excess water and let peas cool.

4

Add tamarind sauce and yogurt to your liking on each serving, and serve sprinkled with *chaat* spices as desired.

Note: For variety and in order to add a little crunch to the preparation, crush a few *golgappe* (hollow crispy wafers) on each serving.

ALOO TIKKI

Potato Cutlets

Serves	6
Preparation time	10 minutes
Cooking time	25 minutes

A *chaat* shop looks rather barren without a big black griddle in a corner with potato cutlets sizzling on it. This preparation can be served as a side dish; it is also suitable for picnics and parties.

Imperial (Metric)	American
1½ lb (675g) potatoes	1½ pounds potatoes
Sea salt, to taste	Sea salt, to taste
3 tablespoonsful chopped onion	3 tablespoons chopped onion
½ teaspoonful grated root ginger	½ teaspoon grated ginger root
2 teaspoonsful garam masala	2 teaspoons garam masala
2 green chillies, chopped	2 green chili peppers, chopped
3 tablespoonsful chopped coriander leaves	3 tablespoons chopped cilantro (coriander)
Wholemeal breadcrumbs, to coat	Whole wheat breadcrumbs, to coat
Ghee, to shallow-fry	Ghee, to shallow-fry

1

Boil the potatoes; then peel and mash them, and divide into 12 portions. Make a small, fat disc of each portion with your hands.

2

Place the salt, onion, ginger, garam masala, chillies and coriander in a suitable bowl, and mix thoroughly. Divide this mixture into 12 portions to serve as filling.

3

Stuff one portion of filling into one disc of potato and flatten into a fat disc. When all the discs are made, roll them in the breadcrumbs.

4

Heat a little ghee on a griddle and position 4 (or more) of these discs on the griddle; turn them over when they are nicely browned and continue cooking until the other side is browned to your liking.

5

Serve hot, freshly made, with a chutney or whatever you fancy!

ALOO CHAAT

Potato in Tamarind Sauce

Serves	6
Preparation time	15 minutes
Cooking time	10 minutes

If you like potatoes, this could be the quickest *chaat* dish you ever made! For variety, you may serve it with lemon juice instead of chutney.

Imperial (Metric)	American
6 medium-sized potatoes	6 medium-sized potatoes
Tamarind sauce	Tamarind sauce
Yogurt, whisked with water, to serve	Yogurt, whisked with water, to serve
Usual *chaat* spices (sea salt, cayenne pepper, ground cumin) to serve	Usual *chaat* spices (sea salt, cayenne pepper, ground cumin) to serve

1

Place the potatoes with enough water to cover in a saucepan, and bring to a boil. Cook until tender.

2

Peel the potatoes and cut into round slices.

3

Pour some tamarind sauce and yogurt over each serving, and sprinkle with the spices as desired.

4

Serve, to be eaten with cocktail sticks (toothpicks) or spoons.

ALOO DHANIAWAALE

Potatoes in Green Sauce

Serves 6	
Preparation time 15 minutes	
Cooking time 10 minutes	

You can rustle up this snack dish in no time at all. Your guests are sure to be green with envy! Also suitable served as a side dish with a main meal.

Imperial (Metric)	*American*
1 lb (450g) very small new potatoes	1 pound very small new potatoes
5 tablespoonsful fresh coriander leaves	5 tablespoons fresh cilantro (coriander)
2 green chillies	2 green chili peppers
Sea salt, to taste	Sea salt, to taste
4 tablespoonsful fresh lemon juice	¼ cup fresh lemon juice

1

Boil and peel the potatoes. If too big to eat in one bite, cut into convenient pieces.

2

Carefully pierce the potatoes with cocktail sticks (toothpicks), making sure the potatoes are not broken.

3

Finely grind the coriander and chillies; add salt and lemon juice and make a paste. Thickly coat the potatoes and leave them for about 5 minutes, to allow the mixture to seep in.

4

Serve sprinkled with additional condiments and lemon juice, if desired. This dish is best eaten with cocktail sticks (toothpicks).

ALOO BONDE

Potato Bundles

Serves	6
Preparation time	15 minutes
Cooking time	20 minutes

Another versatile dish. As a *chaat* snack, it is served topped with chutneys and spices; it can also be served with a main meal or with drinks. I enjoy it with a sour chutney.

Imperial (Metric)	American
6 medium-sized potatoes	6 medium-sized potatoes
1 tablespoonful finely chopped onion	1 tablespoon finely chopped onion
Pinch of sea salt	Pinch of sea salt
2 green chillies, chopped	2 green chili peppers, chopped
Pinch of grated, fresh ginger root	Pinch of grated, fresh ginger root
½ teaspoonful garam masala	½ teaspoon garam masala
1 tablespoonful chopped coriander leaves	1 tablespoon chopped cilantro (coriander)
4 oz (100g) chick pea flour	1 cup chick pea flour
Water, as necessary	Water, as necessary
Vegetable oil, for deep-frying	Vegetable oil, for deep-frying
Usual *chaat* chutneys and spices	Usual *chaat* chutneys and spices

1

Boil the potatoes; then peel and mash them.

2

Add the onion, salt, chillies, ginger, garam masala and coriander to the potato and mash together. Divide the mixture into 12 portions and make a round ball from each.

3

Place the chick pea flour in a deep bowl. Add water as necessary to make a medium batter.

4

Heat sufficient oil in a *kadhai* or deep fryer.

5

Take a potato ball, dip it well into the batter to coat, and deep-fry in the oil — make 4 to 6 at a time. When they are cooked with brown spots around them, remove and drain on paper towels. Serve with a chutney of your choice; they taste better when hot.

CHAAT BAIGANEE

Aubergine (Eggplant) Fritters

Serves 6
Preparation time   10 minutes
Cooking time   20 minutes

Some *chaat* shops in India make a special feature of this dish. The fritters are usually long in shape and heavily coated in batter; the usual *chaat* spices and chutneys give *baiganees* a whole new dimension.

4 oz (100g) chick pea flour	1 cup chick pea flour
4 oz (100g) black bean powder	1 cup black bean powder
Pinch of asafoetida powder	Pinch of asafoetida powder
Pinch of baking powder	Pinch of baking powder
Water, as necessary	Water, as necessary
3 long aubergines	3 long eggplants
Vegetable oil, for deep-frying	Vegetable oil, for deep-frying
Usual *chaat* chutneys and spices	Usual *chaat* chutneys and spices

1

Mix and rub together the chick pea flour, black bean powder, asafoetida powder and baking powder in a bowl. Add water as necessary to make a thick batter.

2

Wash and clean the aubergines (eggplants) and cut into long slices.

3

Heat sufficient oil in a *kadhai* or a deep fryer.

4

Cover the aubergine (eggplant) slices thickly in batter and deep-fry, 4 to 6 at a time, until deep golden all over. Take them out, and drain on paper towels.

5

Serve topped with chutneys and spice powders as desired.

PAALAK KI CHAAT

Spinach Fritters

Serves	4
Preparation time	10 minutes
Cooking time	10 minutes

This dish, also known as *paalaki*, is usually served cold. It is crisp and tasty. Feel free to experiment with other leafy vegetables.

Imperial (Metric)	American
2 oz (50g) chick pea flour	½ cup chick pea flour
Water, as necessary	Water, as necessary
Vegetable oil, for deep-frying	Vegetable oil, for deep-frying
4 oz (100g) fresh young spinach leaves	2 cups fresh, young spinach leaves
Usual *chaat* chutneys and spices	Usual *chaat* chutneys and spices

1

Place the chick pea flour in a deep bowl and, adding water as necessary, make a thin batter.

2

Heat sufficient oil in a *kadhai* or a deep fryer.

3

Take a whole spinach leaf, dip it well into the batter to coat, and carefully slide into the *kadhai*. Keep turning over until golden on both sides; make 3 or 4 at a time. When cooked, remove the *paalakis* and drain on paper towels.

4

Add the usual chutneys on each serving and sprinkle with condiments as desired.

GOLGAPPE

Hollow Crispy Wafers

Serves 6
Preparation time 10 minutes plus 30 minutes standing time
Cooking time 20 minutes

Golgappe, the plural of *golgappa*, are also known as *paani ke bataashe*. They are very light on the stomach. A certain skill is required to eat them; each one has to be eaten in one mouthful as soon as it is filled!

Imperial (Metric)	American
4 oz (100g) wholemeal flour	1 cup whole wheat flour
2 oz (50g) black bean powder	½ cup black bean powder
Ghee, as necessary	Ghee, as necessary
Water, as necessary	Water, as necessary
2 boiled potatoes, peeled and chopped	2 boiled potatoes, peeled and chopped
Cumin sauce, for filling	Cumin sauce, for filling
Sea salt and chilli powder, as required	Sea salt and chili powder, as required

1

Sift the flour and bean powder into a bowl and rub in 2 teaspoons ghee. Adding water as necessary, make a stiff dough. Cover with a damp cloth and let stand about 30 minutes.

2

Knead again and roll out the entire dough into a thin, round disc. Using a bottle cap, cut out 1-inch/2.5cm discs from the dough. Keep them covered with a damp cloth.

3

In a *kadhai* or a deep-fryer, heat sufficient ghee and deep fry these small discs — a few at a time — until they puff up and are nicely brown all over. In order to help the discs puff up, stand a stirrer up in the middle of the *kadhai* and shake gently to make waves in the ghee. When cooked, drain the *golgappe* carefully (making sure you do not crack or smash them) on paper towels.

4

Make a hole in the top of the *golgappa* with a finger, fill with boiled potato and cumin sauce (sprinkle with sea salt and chilli powder if desired), and serve one at a time.

KHASTA CHAAT

Stuffed Discs

Serves	4
Preparation time	20 minutes
Cooking time	35 minutes

This sumptuous dish is the shredded wheat of the *chaat* shop; two of these are usually enough for anyone! They are filling and extremely delicious.

Imperial (Metric)	American
Section A	**Section A**
8 oz (225g) wholemeal flour	2 cups whole wheat flour
Pinch of sea salt	Pinch of sea salt
4 tablespoonsful, ghee	4 tablespoons ghee
Water, as necessary	Water, as necessary
Section B	**Section B**
2 teaspoonsful white cumin seeds	2 teaspoons white cumin seeds
1 tablespoonful ghee	1 tablespoon ghee
Pinch of asafoetida powder	Pinch of asafoetida powder
½ teaspoonful garam masala	½ teaspoon garam masala
Coarsely grind:	Coarsely grind:
4 oz (100g) dried black beans	½ cup dried black beans
1 teaspoonful coriander seeds	1 teaspoon coriander seeds
4 black peppercorns	4 black peppercorns
2 cloves	2 cloves
Water, as necessary	Water, as necessary
Section C	**Section C**
Ghee, for deep-frying	Ghee, for deep-frying
1 boiled potato, peeled and diced	1 boiled potato, peeled and diced
Usual *chaat* chutneys and spices	Usual *chaat* chutneys and spices

1

Rub the flour with the salt and ghee in a bowl. Adding water as necessary, knead into a stiff dough. Divide into 8 portions; roll and flatten each one by hand into a small, fat disc. Cover with a damp cloth, and let the dough rest while you prepare the stuffing.

2

Place the cumin in a *kadhai* or frying pan and sauté it in ghee until it changes colour. Then stir in the asafoetida and garam masala and blend. Add coarsely ground ingredients, some water and stir thoroughly. Cook about 10 minutes; then remove from heat and let cool. Divide this mixture into 8 portions.

3

Take one disc of dough; place one portion of the stuffing on it, fold and flatten by hand. Then roll out into a thin disc. Prepare all 8 discs similarly.

4

Heat sufficient ghee in a *kadhai* or a deep fryer and deep-fry the discs — 4 at a time — over low heat — about 10 minutes. When nicely light brown all over, remove from pan and place on paper towels to drain off excess oil.

5

To serve, make a hole on the top of the *khasta* and put in some potato. Spoon some chutney and yogurt mixture over the *khasta* and serve sprinkled with condiments as desired.

Chapter 11

Meethe Pakwaan
Indian Sweets

Indians adore sweets. Every happy occasion or religious festival is an event for offering and receiving sweets. The fact that India is the third largest producer of sugar in the world serves only as a further stimulus to the Indian tendency to talk about (and eat) sweets at the slightest provocation. There are innumerable religious festivals and occasions; there are birthdays, marriages and happy examination and service competition results; on these occasions, it is almost obligatory for hosts to "sweeten the mouths" of their friends and members of the family. Thus, roughly every day of the year is a "sweets day" for the Indians! In addition, sweets are also offered to bribe and pamper the children and placate the gods.

Indians make an almost infinite number of sweets; there are, of course, a huge range of specialities from every region, and many become national sweets because they are liked by all. Very many Indian sweets are milk-based and are made from milk or milk-derived basic ingredients like *kheers* and *khoya* dishes. Many dishes are made from wholemeal and other flours like chick pea flour; others are made from *dhals* and *dhal*-derived basic ingredients. Coconut contributes substantially to the gigantic repertoire of Indian sweets. Sweet dishes are also made from fruits and vegetables.

As this book in its limited size seeks to cover the whole gamut of Indian vegetarian cookery, I can only offer a few examples of Indian sweets. Given the obvious space constraints, I hope and believe that you will find the selection of recipes offered both educational and enjoyable.

KHOYA PEDA

Sweet Flat Cake

Serves	4
Preparation time	10 minutes
Cooking time	15 minutes

Nothing could be simpler to make! Adjust the quantity of sugar to your liking. Serve before or after a meal, or quite independently, when the mood takes you.

Imperial (Metric)	American
1 lb (450g) freshly made *khoya*	1 pound freshly made *khoya*
8 oz (225g) raw cane sugar	1 cup raw sugar
1 teaspoonful rose water	1 teaspoon rose water
1 tablespoonful chopped pistachios	1 tablespoon chopped pistachio nuts

1

Place the *khoya* in a *kadhai* or a saucepan and put it over low heat. With a metal *karchhi*, stir the khoya about and sauté it properly until the moisture has evaporated and the *khoya* has become dark gold in colour.

2

Remove pan from heat. Add sugar and mix thoroughly. Sprinkle with rose water and mix again. Then let the mixture cool.

3

Pluck small portions from the khoya mixture and mould by hand (wetting and washing the palms of your hands with warm water as necessary) into flat, round tablet shapes.

4

Drop a few chopped pistachios on each tablet and press lightly with a thumb to ensure that they stick to the *pedas*.

5

Serve hot or cold. Store in a dry, cool place for later use.

KHAJOOR

Sweet Nuggets

Serves 4

Preparation time 15 minutes plus 30 minutes standing time

Cooking time 25 minutes

This is a stylish sweet snack; it can be cooked and stored in advance. Quite suitable for picnics and elevenses.

Imperial (Metric)	American
4 oz (100g) wholemeal flour	1 cup whole wheat flour
Ghee, as necessary	Ghee, as necessary
2 oz (50g) raw cane sugar	¼ cup raw sugar
Water, as necessary	Water, as necessary
4 oz (100g) finely chopped nuts of your choice (cashews, almonds and/or chironji or melon seeds)	1 cup finely chopped nuts of your choice (cashews, almonds and/or chironji or melon seeds)

1

Mix the flour, 4 tablespoons ghee and sugar in a bowl and rub together thoroughly. Add water as necessary and knead into a stiff dough. Cover with a damp cloth and let stand for about 30 minutes.

2

Divide the dough into 8 portions. Roll each portion into a ball and flatten into an oval shape — but not too thin. Then press each with a fork; alternatively, make a design or several incisions with a knife on one side of the nugget.

3

Place the chopped nuts on a flat dish. Roll each nugget in the nuts and press lightly.

4

Heat sufficient ghee in a *kadhai* or a deep fryer. Deep-fry the nut-studded nuggets, over very low heat, until golden brown. Remove, when cooked, and place on paper towels to drain off excess oil.

5

Serve hot or cold.

MEETHI BOONDI

Sweet Batter Drops

Serves	4
Preparation time	10 minutes
Cooking time	40 minutes

This is an attractive sweet dish which can be made quickly. The two main items, batter drops (*boondi*) and the syrup (*chaashni*), can be made separately in advance. Those with a sweet tooth will love it!

Imperial (Metric)	American
4 oz (100g) chick pea flour	1 cup chick pea flour
Water, as necessary	Water, as necessary
Pinch of baking powder	Pinch of baking powder
Small pinch of turmeric	Small pinch of turmeric
Ghee, for deep-frying	Ghee, for deep-frying
8 oz (225g) raw cane sugar	1 cup raw sugar
½ pint (300ml) water	1¼ cups water
Pinch of saffron	Pinch of saffron
Kewra water, to serve*	Kewra water, to serve*

*Obtainable as an essence from Indian (speciality) stores.

1

Mix together in a deep bowl the chick pea flour, baking powder and turmeric. Gradually add water as necessary to make a thin batter of "drop" consistency.

2

Heat sufficient ghee in a *kadhai* or a deep frying pan. Place a slotted spoon (with large perforations) across the pan and pour the batter over it; small drops of batter will fall into the ghee. Keep the heat at moderate, move the spoon around the pan, and make as many drops (*boondi*) as you can in one go. When deep golden, remove and drain on paper towels.

3

Place the sugar and water in a saucepan and cook over moderate heat until you have a "1-string" syrup. Add saffron and remove pan from heat.

4

Add the drops to the syrup and soak for about 5 minutes.

5

Serve hot, with additional syrup as needed, after squirting each serving with kewra water.

SHAKAR PAARE

Sweet Flour Puffs

Serves	4
Preparation time	15 minutes
Cooking time	30 minutes

These are also known as *meethe kurme* and are cooked and stored in advance. Adults enjoy nibbling at them to cure in-between meal peckishness; children need no excuse! Good for picnics and parties, too.

Imperial (Metric)	American
8 oz (225g) wholemeal flour	2 cups whole wheat flour
Small pinch of sea salt	Small pinch of sea salt
3 tablespoonsful double cream	3 tablespoons heavy cream
Ghee, as necessary	Ghee, as necessary
Water, as necessary	Water, as necessary
1 pint (600ml) 2-string raw cane sugar syrup	2½ cups 2-string raw sugar syrup
Pinch of ground cardamom	Pinch of ground cardamom

1

Sift the flour and salt into a deep bowl. Add the cream and 4 tablespoons ghee and rub the mixture together. Adding water as necessary, knead into a stiff dough of crumbly texture.

2

Mould the dough into a ball and roll it out into a round disc about ½ inch/1.25cm thick. Using a sharp knife, cut this disc into diamond or square shapes.

3

Heat sufficient ghee in a *kadhai*, or a deep fryer, and cook the dough over low heat until golden. When cooked, remove and place on paper towels to drain.

4

Reheat the sugar syrup and add the cardamom. When the syrup is hot, immerse the puffs and leave them over very low heat for 5 minutes.

5

Remove from heat when puffs are well-soaked and well-coated, and let them cool.

6

Separate them from each other with a knife or fork and store in a covered container. Serve as required.

CHHOHAARE KI BURFI

Dried Date Toffee

Serves 6

Preparation time 10 minutes

Cooking time 15 minutes

This sweet dish owes it origins to the Gujrat state of India and has a large following. I hope that it will recruit some patrons among westerners, too.

Imperial (Metric)	American
8 oz (225g) stoned dried dates, finely chopped	3 cups minced, pitted, dried dates,
4 oz (100g) *khoya*	¼ pound *khoya*
4 oz (100g) raw cane sugar (or to taste)	½ cup raw sugar (or to taste)
4 tablespoonsful ghee	4 tablespoons ghee
4 oz (100g) mixed dried fruits and nuts (green cardamom pods, chironji or melon seeds, almonds and sultanas), chopped	1 cup mixed dried fruits and nuts (green cardamom pods, chironji or melon seeds, almonds and golden seedless raisins), chopped
1 teaspoonful rose water	1 teaspoon rose water
Edible silver foil, to serve	Edible silver foil, to serve

1

Sauté the dates in a saucepan in 1 tablespoon ghee over low heat — for about 3 minutes. Add the *khoya*, sugar and half the dried fruits and nuts until mixture thickens. Then add almost all the remaining ghee (reserving a little for greasing the plate) and continue cooking until ghee separates.

2

Grease a large plate with reserved ghee and scatter remaining dried fruits and nuts over it. Remove pan from heat and pour the contents over the plate, spreading evenly.

3

Sprinkle the rose water over the mixture and cut into desired shapes. Turn over and decorate with edible silver foil.

4

Serve as desired.

Note: Leftover toffee can be stored in an airtight container.

GAAJAR HALWA

Shredded Carrot Pudding

Serves	4
Preparation time	15 minutes
Cooking time	35 minutes

This is a popular sweet dish from Northern India. This particular dish can be eaten hot or cold; it can be reheated a second and third time without losing its flavour. For best results, shred the carrots as fine as possible, and as long.

Imperial (Metric)	American
1 lb (450g) tender carrots	1 pound tender carrots
4 oz (100g) ghee	½ cup ghee
½ pint (300ml) milk	1¼ cups milk
6 oz (175g) granulated *khoya*	1 cup granulated *khoya*
6 oz (175g) raw cane sugar (or to taste)	1 cup raw sugar (or to taste)
1 tablespoonful flaked almonds	1 tablespoon slivered almonds
Pinch of coarsely ground green cardamom seeds	Pinch of coarsely ground green cardamom seeds
Pinch of saffron	Pinch of saffron
1 teaspooonful kewra water	1 teaspoon kewra water
Edible silver foil, to decorate	Edible silver foil, to decorate

1

Wash, scrape, and grate the carrots finely.

2

Heat the ghee in a *kadhai* or a saucepan and sauté the carrots over low heat for about 5 minutes; keep the pan covered and stir once or twice.

3

Add the milk, increase heat to medium, and bring to a boil. Mix in *khoya*, lower heat, and cook until milk is fully absorbed into carrots and is well blended with the khoya, stirring occasionally — about 20 minutes.

4

Stir in the sugar and let it dissolve. Add the almonds and cardamom pods.

5

Remove from heat; add saffron and kewra, and stir a few times.

6

Garnish with edible silver foil and serve hot or cold.
Note: Any leftover halwa can be kept in the refrigerator. Reheat before using if desired.

BESAN KA HALWA

Chick Pea Flour Pudding

Serves 4
Preparation time 10 minutes
Cooking time 15 minutes

Halwas are normally served in India at breakfast time; they can be made with different flours and thus they offer you scope for experimentation. They are made in no time!

Imperial (Metric)	*American*
4 oz (100g) ghee	½ cupful ghee
4 oz (100g) chick pea flour	1 cup chick pea flour
¼ pint (150ml) water	⅔ cup water
4 oz (100g) raw cane sugar (or to taste)	½ cup raw sugar (or to taste)
2 oz (50g) chopped nuts (pistachios, almonds and cashews)	½ cup chopped nuts (pistachios, almonds and cashews)
Pinch of ground cardamom	Pinch of ground cardamom

1

Heat the ghee in a *kadhai*, or a saucepan, and sauté the chick pea flour about 5 minutes over low heat; keep stirring. Make sure that the flour is cooked and wait for an aromatic smell to develop before continuing to the next stage.

2

Add water; stir constantly to avoid the formation of lumps in the flour. When water is fully absorbed, add sugar and half the nuts and blend thoroughly. Continue stirring until the mixture becomes thick.

3

Remove pan from heat, stir in remaining nuts and serve hot, sprinkled with the cardamom.

ALOO KI KHEER

Potato Pudding

Serves	4
Preparation time	10 minutes
Cooking time	25 minutes

Indian *kheers*, somewhat similar to milk puddings, occupy an exalted position in the annals of Indian cuisine. For presentation, most *kheers* are served decorated with pounded edible silver or gold foil.

Imperial (Metric)	American
1 tablespoonful ghee	1 tablespoon ghee
2 medium-sized potatoes, scraped and grated	2 medium-sized potatoes, scraped and grated
2 pints (1.15 litres) milk	5 cups milk
4 oz (100g) raw cane sugar (or to taste)	½ cup raw sugar (or to taste)
4 green cardamom pods	4 green cardamom pods
1 teaspoonful flaked almonds	1 teaspoon slivered almonds
1 teaspoonful chopped pistachios	1 teaspoon chopped pistachios
Rose water, to serve	Rose water, to serve
Edible silver foil, to decorate	Edible silver foil, to decorate

1

Heat the ghee in a *kadhai* or frying pan and sauté the potato until deep golden. Remove from heat and drain on paper towels.

2

Pour the milk into a deep saucepan and cook over moderate heat. After the first boil, lower heat and continue cooking until milk thickens.

3

Stir in potatoes and sugar and continue to cook for another 10 minutes. Then add cardamom, almonds and pistachios, and blend thoroughly. Remove from heat and let cool.

4

Serve sprinkled with the rose water and decorated with the edible foil.

LEECHI KI KHEER

Lychee Pudding

Serves	6
Preparation time	10 minutes
Cooking time	35 minutes

Lychee fruit is available in season from Asian fruiterers; or use the tinned variety. The taste of this pudding is out of this world: The proof lies in the eating.

Imperial (Metric)	American
1½ pints (900ml) milk	3¾ cups milk
4 oz (100g) lychee flesh	10 lychee nuts
4 oz (100g) raw cane sugar (or to taste)	½ cup raw sugar (or to taste)
2 oz (50g) chopped nuts of your choice	½ cup chopped nuts of your choice
6 drops kewra essence	6 drops kewra essence
1 teaspoonful ground cardamom	1 teaspoon ground cardamom
½ teaspoonful saffron	½ teaspoon saffron

1

Pour the milk into a saucepan, place over moderate heat and cook until reduced by a quarter.

2

Add the lychee flesh and blend well. Then add the sugar and nuts. Continue cooking, stirring periodically.

3

When milk is reduced to half, remove pan from heat, sprinkle on kewra essence, and let cool.

4

Serve topped with cardamom and garnished with saffron.

SHAAHI TUKRE

Toast for Royalty

Serves 4
Preparation time   10 minutes plus soaking time
Cooking time   10 minutes

This dish converts ordinary bread slices into a delicious and exotic confection; it also offers some scope for experimentation with alternative ingredients.

Imperial (Metric)	American
4 thick wholemeal bread slices	4 thick whole wheat bread slices
Ghee, for deep-frying	Ghee, for deep-frying
5 tablespoonsful 1-string raw	⅓ cup 1-string raw
cane sugar syrup	sugar syrup
4 tablespoonsful double cream	4 tablespoons heavy cream
4 edible gold foils	4 edible gold foils
1 tablespoonful grated nuts (cashews,	1 tablespoon grated nuts (cashews,
almonds and pistachios)	almonds and pistachios)
Pinch of ground cardamom	Pinch of ground cardamom
A few saffron strands	A few saffron strands
Kewra water, to serve	Kewra water, to serve

1

Remove the crusts from the bread and cut each slice into 4 pieces.

2

Heat sufficient ghee in a *kadhai* or a deep frying pan and sauté the bread until golden brown. Remove and place on individual serving dishes.

3

Reheat raw sugar syrup and pour some over each individual serving, reserving a little syrup for later; let bread soak for 10 minutes.

4

Pour 1 tablespoon cream over each serving and let it soak in for 2 minutes.

5

Spread a gold (or silver) foil over each portion and sprinkle the nuts over the foil.

6

Add a little cardamom and about 4 strands of saffron to each portion.

7

Just before serving, pour the remaining syrup evenly over each portion to give it a nice glaze.

8

Serve warm or cold, with a few drops of kewra water on each serving.

TIL PATTI

Sesame Snaps

Serves   6

Preparation time   10 minutes plus approximately 1 hour soaking and drying time
Cooking time   25 minutes

Often served after a main meal as a sweet, this dish is known for its digestive properties. Children love to eat it at any time!

Imperial (Metric)	American
8 oz (225g) white sesame seeds	1½ cups white sesame seeds
8 oz (225g) *gur* (molasses)	1 cup *gur* (molasses)
½ pint (300ml) water	1¼ cups water
Ghee, to grease	Ghee, to grease

1

Clean and wash the sesame seeds and soak for about 30 minutes. Then let seeds dry and lightly sauté on a griddle over low heat.

2

Place the molasses and water in a saucepan and cook over moderate heat until you have a "2-string" syrup — about 20 minutes.

3

Remove from heat, add the sesame seeds to the syrup and mix thoroughly.

4

Grease a large plate and spread mixture evenly over it. Let it cool a little, and cut into desired shapes.

5

This sweet is usually served cold.

Note: The thinner you spread the mixture, the crunchier the sesame snaps will be. Leftovers can be stored in a plastic bag or a jar for later use.

SHRIKHAND

Flavoured Yogurt

Serves   6

Preparation time   10 minutes plus overnight dripping and 30 minutes chilling time

This unique creamy dessert is made all over India, with some regional variations. It is most popular on the western seaboard of India, i.e., the Gujrat and Maharashtra region, where it is served with *puris*.

Imperial (Metric)	American
1½ pints (900ml) natural yogurt	3¾ cups plain yogurt
4 oz (100g) raw cane sugar (or to taste)	½ cup raw sugar (or to taste)
Pinch of crushed saffron, steeped in	Pinch of crushed saffron, steeped
in 1 tablespoonful rose water	in 1 tablespoon rose water
1 tablespoonful chopped nuts	1 tablespoon chopped nuts
(almonds, pistachios and cashews)	(almonds, pistachios, and cashews)
Small pinch each: ground cinnamon	Small pinch each: ground cinnamon
and cardamom	and cardamom
Fresh rose petals, to garnish	Fresh rose petals, to garnish

1

Place the yogurt in a clean muslin cloth, fold it up into a loose bundle, and hang overnight; the moisture will drip through.

2

Transfer yogurt to a bowl; stir in sugar and steeped saffron, and whisk mixture thoroughly.

3

Add the nuts, together with cinnamon and cardamom, and whisk again until mixture assumes a smooth consistency.

4

Garnish with rose petals and chill for about 30 minutes before serving.

ALOO MURABBA

Preserved Potatoes

Serves 6
Preparation time 15 minutes
Cooking time 30 minutes

Sweetmeats of this type last a long time; they come in handy when you wish to serve a sweet to an unexpected guest and the shops are closed. *Murabbas* are good for the brain and possess cooling properties.

Imperial (Metric)	American
6 medium-sized potatoes	6 medium-sized potatoes
Water, as necessary	Water, as necessary
1 tablespoonful lemon juice	1 tablespoon lemon juice
1½ pints (900ml) 1-string raw cane sugar syrup	3¾ cups 1-string raw sugar syrup
Pinch of ground cardamom	Pinch of ground cardamom
Pinch of crushed saffron	Pinch of crushed saffron
Edible silver foil, to serve	Edible silver foil, to serve

1

Peel the potatoes and prick them all over with a fork. Place in a saucepan and add enough water to cover; stir in half the lemon juice. Place the pan over moderate heat and bring to a boil. Remove from the heat and cool. Drain off the water.

2

Place the syrup in a deep saucepan; add the remaining lemon juice and place the pan over low heat. Drop in the potatoes and cook until the syrup thickens — about 20 minutes. Remove pan from heat and let it cool.

3

Stir in cardamom and saffron — taking care not to break the potatoes — and store in a sterilized glass jar.

4

Decorate each serving with an edible silver foil; serve as desired.

ANANNAS MURABBA

Preserved Pineapple

Serves   4

Preparation time   15 minutes plus 2 hours standing time

Cooking time   30 minutes

A popular preserve among the intellectual fraternity, its soothing properties are put to best advantage when served first thing in the morning. Some people make large quantities in advance and serve as required.

Imperial (Metric)	American
1 pineapple (1 lb (450g) ready weight)	1 pineapple (1 pound ready weight)
Water, as necessary	Water, as necessary
1 teaspoonful sea salt	1 teaspoon sea salt
2 oz (50g) edible lime powder	2 ounces edible lime powder
1½ pints (900ml) 1-string raw cane sugar syrup	3¾ cups 1-string raw sugar syrup
1 tablespoonful fresh lemon juice	1 tablespoon fresh lemon juice
Edible silver foil, to serve	Edible silver foil, to serve

1

Cut the rind off the pineapple with a sharp knife.

2

Make a paste by adding sufficient water to the salt and lime powder. Smear this paste on the outside of the pineapple and stand on a strainer about 2 hours, so that liquid drains off.

3

Thoroughly but carefully wash the pineapple in several changes of clear water. Then, with a fork, prick the pineapple all over — making sure it does not break.

4

Place the pineapple in a saucepan with enough water to cover; put it over moderate heat and bring to a boil. Drain and put on a large plate.

5

Pour the sugar syrup into a large saucepan and stir in lemon juice; add pineapple and cook over low heat until syrup thickens. Remove from heat and cool.

6

Store in a large, sterilized covered container. Cut and serve as required; decorate each serving with an edible gold or silver foil.

Chapter 12

Sharbat, Chuskiyaan aur Kulfi
Cold Drinks, Lollies and Ice Creams

Indians pride themselves on the bewildering variety of cold soft drinks they can offer. A wide range of fresh fruit grows in India throughout the year and a glass of freshly made *sharbat* goes down as a treat in the early evening breeze after a sweltering summer day! A small selection of fashionable *sharbats* is offered in this section.

Warm weather demands cold offerings; *sharbats* are not the only coolers Indian hosts offer their guests. *Chuskis* — of which lollies (popsicles) are the rough western equivalent — in many varieties are made in India throughout the summer months (normally from April to August); they are the particular favourites of students — young and old alike. A few of these have been included in this chapter.

Kulfi — the scrumptious queen of the Indian ice creams — is as yet an almost undiscovered phenomenon of the Indian cuisine in the West; the West does not know what it is missing! Kulfi is of a harder consistency than western ice cream; it is a rich and rather classy concoction. The traditional way of making *kulfi* is to pour boiled milk into conical tin moulds with tight-fitting lids, then freeze it by immersing these moulds in a large earthen pitcher full of ice and salt. But plastic ice cube trays (or other suitable containers) and modern freezers do an equally efficient job!

SEB SAROVAR

Apple Cooler

Serves 6
Preparation time 5 minutes
Cooking time 15 minutes

Intellectuals are partial to this drink; I hope everyone likes it! Serve chilled.

Imperial (Metric)	American
3 sweet apples, peeled, cored and diced	3 sweet apples, pared, cored and diced
1 tablespoonful pineapple juice	1 tablespoon pineapple juice
1 teaspoonful fresh lemon juice	1 teaspoon fresh lemon juice
5 tablespoonsful raw cane sugar	1/3 cup raw sugar
1½ pints (900ml) water	3¾ cups water
Crushed ice, to serve	Crushed ice, to serve
Rose water, to serve	Rose water, to serve

1

Place the apples, fruit juices, sugar and water in a saucepan and bring to a boil over medium heat. Cook about 10 minutes.

2

Mash the apples into the liquid to obtain a smooth consistency. Lower heat and cook another 5 minutes.

3

Remove pan from heat, strain purée, and let it cool.

4

Add crushed ice to each serving and serve with a generous sprinkling of rose water.

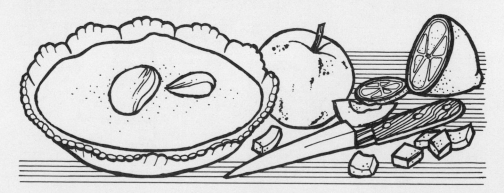

BER KA SHARBAT

Prune Juice

Serves   4
Preparation time   5 minutes plus chilling time
Cooking time   15 minutes

This can turn into a real Oriental delight if you can find the original Indian *bers* (dried plums). It will look good on any table setting!

Imperial (Metric)	American
1 pint (600ml) water	2½ cups water
4 oz (100g) stoned prunes	1 cup pitted prunes
5 tablespoonsful raw cane sugar	⅓ cup raw sugar
Pinch of sea salt	Pinch of sea salt
Small pinch of ground nutmeg	Small pinch of ground nutmeg
Pinch of ground cinnamon	Pinch of ground cinnamon
Squeeze of lemon juice	Squeeze of lemon juice
Crushed ice, to serve	Crushed ice, to serve

1

Place the water in a saucepan and bring to a boil. Add the prunes and continue to cook over low heat for another 10 minutes.

2

Remove pan from heat; mash prunes into water, push purée through a sieve, and let it cool.

3

Add the rest of the ingredients, except ice, whisk thoroughly, and chill.

4

Serve in long, tapering glasses, topped with ice.

RASBHARI MADHUSHAALA

Raspberry Lovey-Dovey

Serves 6

Preparation time 5 minutes plus chilling time

This drink refreshes you all over! Make it with ripe Indian *rasbharis*.

Imperial (Metric)	American
3 tablespoonsful raspberry juice	3 tablespoons raspberry juice
1 tablespoonful raspberry essence	1 tablespoon raspberry extract
½ teaspoonful clear honey	½ teaspoon clear honey
3 tablespoonsful raw cane sugar	3 tablespoons raw sugar
1½ pints (900ml) cold milk	3¾ cups cold milk
1 teaspoonful kewra water	1 teaspoon kewra water
Crushed ice, to serve	Crushed ice, to serve

1

Place all the ingredients except the ice in a liquidizer and blend thoroughly (or use a hand whisk).

2

Serve chilled, topped with ice.

PHAALSE KA SHARBAT

Blackberry Downpour

Serves 4

Preparation time 10 minutes plus overnight soaking and 30 minutes chilling time

This drink fights the heat and purifies the blood; it conjures up images of palm trees, sandy beaches and the sea breeze and is well worth waiting for!

Imperial (Metric)	American
8 oz (225g) blackberries	2 cups blackberries
1 pint (600ml) water	2½ cups water
Raw cane sugar, to taste	Raw sugar, to taste
Small pinch of sea salt	Small pinch of sea salt
Crushed ice, to serve	Crushed ice, to serve
Pineapple slices, to garnish	Pineapple slices, to garnish

1

Soak the blackberries in the measured water overnight.

2

Mash the blackberries into the water, then put the mixture through a sieve.

3

Add sugar and salt and mix thoroughly. Refrigerate the mixture for about 30 minutes.

4

Serve in long glasses, topped with crushed ice and garnished with pineapple.

NAMKEEN LASSI

Savoury Yogurt Cooler

Serves 6
Preparation time   10 minutes plus chilling time

This cold drink has great digestive properties and is delectable! It is quickly made; but you may prefer to chill it before serving.

Imperial (Metric)	American
16 fl oz (480ml) natural yogurt	2 cups plain yogurt
1½ pints (900ml) cold water	3¾ cups cold water
1 teaspoonful sea salt	1 teaspoon sea salt
1 tablespoonful mint leaves, shredded	1 tablespoon mint leaves, shredded
1 tablespoonful white cumin seeds, roasted and ground	1 tablespoon white cumin seeds, roasted and ground
Crushed ice, to serve	Crushed ice, to serve

1

Place the yogurt and water in an appropriate-sized bowl and add the salt, mint and half the ground cumin. Whisk thoroughly until the top of the mixture is quite frothy; alternatively, use a blender. Then chill the mixture.

2

Take 6 long glasses and drop in a generous quantity of crushed ice. Then pour in the frothy mixture.

3

Sprinkle the remaining cumin on each serving.

CHAAY TARAAWAT

Iced Tea

Serves	6
Preparation time	10 minutes
Cooking time	15 minutes

Middle-class Indian homes frequently offer iced tea to their guests these days, although most tea preparations in India are of the hot variety. Whether hot or cold, Indian tea is admired by all civilized palates!

Imperial (Metric)	American
3 tablespoonsful Darjeeling tea	3 tablespoons Darjeeling tea
1½ pints (900ml) water	3¾ cups water
Raw cane sugar, to taste	Raw sugar, to taste
2 tablespoonsful lemon juice	2 tablespoons lemon juice
Crushed ice, to serve	Crushed ice, to serve
Orange slices, to garnish	Orange slices, to garnish

1

Place the tea, water and sugar in a saucepan and bring to a boil; then remove the pan from the heat and let it cool.

2

Serve in long glasses, sprinkled with 1 teaspoon lemon juice on each serving and a generous quantity of crushed ice; garnish with orange slices.

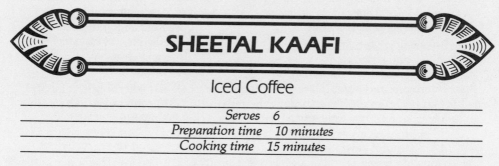

SHEETAL KAAFI

Iced Coffee

Serves	6
Preparation time	10 minutes
Cooking time	15 minutes

This is a fashionable drink, offered in upper middle-class Indian homes. For variety you may serve this cold drink topped with *khoya ki kulfi*.

Imperial (Metric)	American
3 tablespoonsful instant coffee granules	3 tablespoons instant coffee granules
1½ pints (900ml) water	3¾ cups water
3 tablespoonsful raw cane sugar	3 tablespoons raw sugar
(or to taste)	(or to taste)
Pinch of ground cardamom	Pinch of ground cardamom
Crushed ice, to serve	Crushed ice, to serve
12 fl oz (360ml) double cream	1½ cups heavy cream

1

Place the coffee and water in a saucepan and bring to a boil. Add the sugar and cardamom and continue cooking for another 2 minutes over medium heat.

2

Remove saucepan from heat and let it cool.

3

Half fill 6 tall glasses with crushed ice and pour the cool coffee mixture into each glass. Serve topped with cream.

 # PHALON KI CHUSKI

Fruity Ice Lolly

Serves 4
Preparation time   15 minutes plus freezing time

This is an interesting preparation that is open to experimentation. Children will adore it!

Imperial (Metric)	American
2 ripe bananas, chopped	2 ripe bananas, chopped
1 sweet apple, peeled, cored and chopped	1 sweet apple, pared, cored and chopped
segments of satsumas, skinned with pips removed	2 satsuma segments, skinned, with seeds removed
4 oz (100g) seedless grapes	1 cup seedless grapes
1 tablespoonful raw cane sugar	1 tablespoon raw sugar
½ pint (300ml) water	1¼ cups water
1 teaspoonful kewra water	1 teaspoon kewra water

1

Mix the bananas, apple, satsuma, grapes and sugar — and beat thoroughly. Add the water and kewra and whisk again.

2

Pour this mixture into moulds or ice cube trays and freeze on sticks. Serve frozen.

TARBOOZ KI CHUSKI

Watermelon Ice Lolly

Serves 4

Preparation time 5 minutes plus freezing time

Chuskis are firmer than *kulfis* because they are basically obtained by freezing fruit juices and/or water. However, they have their own exotic taste which pleases everyone!

Imperial (Metric)	American
½ pint (300ml) freshly squeezed watermelon juice	1¼ cups freshly squeezed watermelon juice
3 tablespoonsful raw cane sugar (or to taste)	3 tablespoons raw sugar (or to taste)
Small pinch of sea salt	Small pinch of sea salt
½ teaspoonful lemon juice	½ teaspoon lemon juice
½ teaspoonful rose water	½ teaspoon rose water

1

Place all the ingredients in a suitable bowl; whisk thoroughly.

2

Pour the mixture into moulds or ice cube trays and freeze, with or without sticks.

3

If frozen without sticks, serve in contrasting coloured bowls.

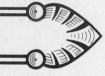

LEECHI KI CHUSKI

Lychee Ice Lolly

Serves 4

Preparation time 5 minutes plus freezing time

Fresh lychees are easily obtainable in the West; so get peeling and freeze the *chuskis* on sticks! Children will love this frozen treat, and so will you.

Imperial (Metric)	American
4 oz (100g) lychee flesh	10 lychees
1 tablespoonful raw cane sugar	1 tablespoon raw sugar
(or to taste)	(or to taste)
½ pint (300ml) water	1¼ cups water
Small pinch of ground cardamom	Small pinch of ground cardamom
4 drops kewra essence	4 drops kewra essence

1

Mix the lychees, sugar and water in a bowl. Whisk briskly by hand; alternatively, use a blender. Add cardamom and kewra and whisk, or blend, a little more.

2

Pour the liquid into moulds or ice cube trays and freeze, with or without sticks.

3

Serve frozen.

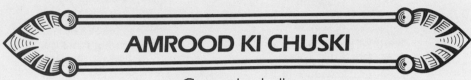

AMROOD KI CHUSKI

Guava Ice Lolly

Serves 4
Preparation time 5 minutes plus freezing time

A magical ice lolly from the mysterious East; an exotic temperature cooler indeed!

Imperial (Metric)	American
2 ripe guavas, peeled and mashed	2 ripe guavas, peeled and mashed
3 tablespoonsful raw cane sugar	3 tablespoons raw sugar
(or to taste)	(or to taste)
½ pint (300ml) water	1¼ cups water
½ teaspoonful rose water	½ teaspoon rose water
Small pinch of sea salt	Small pinch of sea salt

1

Place the guava flesh and sugar in a suitable bowl and whisk together for 2 minutes. Add the remaining ingredients and blend thoroughly.

2

Pour this mixture into moulds or ice cube trays and freeze on sticks.

3

Serve frozen.

KHOYA KI KULFI

Dried Milk Ice Cream

Serves   4
Preparation time   5 minutes
Cooking time   20 minutes plus freezing time

This ice cream should delight young and old alike; it is very suitable for warm summer afternoons.

Imperial (Metric)	American
1 pint (600ml) creamy milk	2½ cups milk or half and half
8 oz (255g) *khoya*	½ pound *khoya*
4 oz (100g) raw cane sugar	⅔ cup raw sugar
(or to taste)	(or to taste)
Pinch of sea salt	Pinch of sea salt
½ teaspoonful ground cardamom	½ teaspoon ground cardamom
8 strands saffron, steeped in	8 strands saffron, steeped in
1 tablespoonful kewra water	1 tablespoon kewra water

1

Boil the milk in a saucepan over medium heat. Lower heat; add the *khoya* and sugar and continue cooking another 10 minutes.

2

Remove pan from heat, stir in remaining ingredients and let the mixture cool.

3

Fill moulds or ice cube trays with this mixture and freeze; when frozen, transfer *kulfis* to a refrigerator. Serve chilled.

KELA KI KULFI

Banana Ice Cream

Serves   4
Preparation time   5 minutes
Cooking time   20 minutes plus freezing time

A delicious *kulfi* indeed! You may experiment with other fruits of your choice and produce stunning ice creams.

Imperial (Metric)	American
1 pint (600ml) creamy milk	2½ cups milk or half and half
4 oz (100g) raw cane sugar	½ cup raw sugar
Pinch of sea salt	Pinch of sea salt
3 tablespoonful rose water	3 tablespoons rose water
2 large, ripe bananas, mashed	2 large, ripe bananas, mashed
½ pint (300ml) double cream	1¼ cups heavy cream

1

Put the milk, sugar, salt and rose water in a saucepan and place over medium heat. Cook until the milk is reduced to half.

2

Remove the pan from the heat; add bananas and cream, and blend thoroughly.

3

When cool, pour the mixture into containers or moulds and freeze. Then transfer to the refrigerator. Serve chilled, when desired.

KAAFI KI KULFI

Coffee Ice Cream

Serves 4
Preparation time 15 minutes
Cooking time 10 minutes plus freezing time

This delicious *kulfi* brings the twains — the East and West — that much closer together!

Imperial (Metric)	American
½ pint (300ml) hot, milky coffee	1¼ cups hot, milky coffee
8 fl oz (240ml) single cream	1 cup light cream
Raw cane sugar, to taste	Raw sugar, to taste
1 teaspoonful rose water	1 teaspoon rose water
Small pinch of sea salt	Small pinch of sea salt

1

Mix all the ingredients together in a suitable bowl and whisk briskly.

2

Transfer the contents to a saucepan and cook over a moderate heat for about 10 minutes. Remove pan from heat and let it cool.

3

Fill containers with the mixture and freeze; then transfer to a refrigerator. Serve chilled.

NEEBU KI KULFI

Lemon Ice Cream

Serves 4
Preparation time   5 minutes
Cooking time   30 minutes plus freezing time

A truly exquisite dessert! You may, if you wish, substitute orange zest and juice for the lemon.

Imperial (Metric)	American
1 pint (600ml) milk	2½ cups milk
4 oz (100g) raw cane sugar	½ cup raw sugar
Grated rind of 1 lemon	Grated rind of 1 lemon
3 tablespoonsful fresh lemon juice	3 tablespoons fresh lemon juice
¼ pint (150ml) double cream	⅔ cup heavy cream
Kewra water, to serve	Kewra water, to serve

1

Mix the milk and sugar in a saucepan; put over medium heat and bring to a boil. Then lower the heat and continue to cook until the milk is reduced to half — about 20 minutes.

2

Place the grated lemon rind in a bowl and pour the cooked milk over it. Add the lemon juice to the cream in a separate bowl and whisk thoroughly. Then pour into the bowl with the cooked milk. Blend the contents well and let the mixture cool.

3

Fill moulds or containers with the mixture and freeze. Serve chilled, sprinkled with kewra water.

Namaste, Phir Milenge

Farewell

After the meal has finished and the empty plates have been removed, when the hostess wafts into the dining room to serve *paan-supaadi*, it denotes the formal conclusion of an Indian meal. The guests each pick up a *paan* and, placing it in their mouths, bid goodbye to their hosts and make for their "carriages" — smiling all over their faces and licking their lips.

The *paan* served to the guests is usually in the form of a *beeda* (a folded up *paan* leaf). The *paan* leaf is first smeared with a layer each of lime paste and *katechu*, after which the desired amount of chopped betel nuts and a variety of other sweet and scented ingredients are heaped on the leaf; it is then folded up into a triangular or round shape and served after being secured with a clove. Often the *beeda* is decorated with edible silver or gold foil, which reportedly adds to the *paan's* already considerable digestive properties. In addition, *paan* refreshes the breath and makes the lips red. *Paans* and their allied ingredients are now available with relative ease in many countries in the West.

The *paan* is a heart-shaped leaf which grows on a creeper; it is usually about 4 inches/10cm in length. *Paan* leaves are of many kinds: the hard, crumbly and delicious variety grown in Mahoba, or the yellow leaves from Varanasi which cater to *paan* connoisseurs as well as novices, the bitter-tasting green leaves from Bengal which suit *paan* addicts admirably. The leaves grown in South India are lighter in colour, slightly smaller in size, softer to touch and absolutely scrumptious in taste!

The *supaadi* (betal nut) offers "muscle" to the *beeda* and *katechu* pastes. The betel nut grows on tall, majestic palm trees; it is grated, shredded or chopped by a special cutter known as a *sarauta*. The chopped betel nut is coloured, sweetened and scented in many different ways and is then used in conjunction with plain betel nuts in preparing the *beeda*.

Among the most important ingredients inside a *beeda* besides betel nuts, lime and *katechu*, is green cardamom: a few seeds are put in every *paan*. Indians also eat whole pods of them! Desiccated (dried) coconut is also added; coconut lends a sweet and silky flavour to the *paans*.

Cloves normally wrap up the case! When the *paan* has been folded up, after placing the various ingredients inside, its shape is secured by a clove. Cloves are also sucked on their own, especially to freshen one's breath.

Saunf is a many-splendoured thing of the Indian kitchen pantry. It is served with the *paan* too; sometimes inside a *beeda*, sometimes separately. Thin *saunf* — aniseed — is normally served as it is; either on its own or with desiccated (dried) coconut and green cardamom. Thick *saunf* — fennel — is usually served roasted; either alone or with green cardamom, coconut and betel nuts.

Prepared and unmade *paans* and allied ingredients are kept in an octagonal, concave box with a handle on the top — known as *paandaan*. These boxes are made of silver, brass or aluminium, and are quite magical inside. First, on an inside tray, the *paan* leaves are kept wrapped in a damp cloth. Underneath this tray is a collection of built-in bowls in which the other ingredients of *paan* are kept.

Every street, bazaar and shopping centre in India has at least one shop or stand selling a variety of *paans* and other accessories; a sight almost like the chemists or tobacconists in the West. These shops get a constant flow of customers from the offices, cinemas, hotels and stores. The price of a prepared *paan* (*beeda*) can vary greatly, from a few *paisa* to several hundred *rupees* each!

Paans round off a meal beautifully; their arrival on the scene is the beginning of the "goodbyes" and the departure of guests, which in normal households lasts no more than a few minutes. Interestingly, after the parties and banquets thrown by the Mughal Emperors and the Nawabs, this ceremony lasted for hours! *Paans* on these occasions were served secured with cloves made of solid gold and silver; the cloves were, of course, thrown away before the *paans* entered the eager gullets of the regal guests. And the maids and servants were richer by that many gold and silver cloves! Before my readers start stampeding into India in search of those lucrative jobs, let me be the bearer of sad tidings: Mughal Emperors and Nawabs no longer exist; nor alas, do such jobs!

Useful Addresses
Ingredients for Indian cooking may be ordered by mail from the following companies:

Viniron Ltd
Patak
119 Drumond Street
London NW1

Bombay Emporium
70 Grafton Way
London W1

Harrods Food Dept
Knightsbridge
London SW1

Fortnum and Mason
181 Picadilly
London W1

Spice and Sweet Mahal
135 Lexington Avenue
New York, NY 10016
(212) 683-0900

Oriental House of Sycracuse
1706 Erie Blvd.
East Sycracuse, NY 13210
(315) 555-1212

House of Spices
1086 Maple Avenue
Cherry Hill, NJ 08002
(649) 665-8292

House of Spices
4101 Walnut Street
Philadelphia, PA 19140
(215) 222-1111

House of Spices
Cypress Plaza Shopping Center
10620 FM 1960
West Houston, TX 77070
(713) 955-7693

House of Spices
Keystone Park Shopping Center
13777 N. Central Expressway
Dallas, TX 75243
(214) 783-7544

House of Spices
12223 E. Centralia Road
Lakewood, CA 90715
(213) 860-9919

INDEX